MODERN APPOINTMENT SETTING

MODERN APPOINTMENT SETTING

Prospecting and Phoning for Financial Professionals

Gail B. Goodman

Author photo provided by author

Cover design by Marie Elisa Shanda Veloso
Cover layout by LACreative
Cover photo provided with permission by Dreamstime

ISBN: 978-0-578-55400-6

Printed in the United States of America

*To my mother, **Harriet Busman**,*
who taught me that being successful
at whatever I wanted was always possible.

CONTENTS

INTRODUCTION

FOR MORE THAN THREE DECADES, I HAVE PROVIDED SEMINARS, TRAINING MATERIALS, coaching, and advice to financial professionals, teaching them how to set initial appointments. Having "enough leads" or "enough appointments" has been this industry's challenge for longer than thirty years. Part of the challenge has been the industry's almost obsessive commitment to teaching products and selling, without giving equal time to training prospecting and appointment setting skills. And yet, most advisors fail from a lack of appointments, not a lack of sales.

I've heard it thousands of times: "If I get my guys in the door, they're terrific. We have a high closing rate." I always respond—"That's the easy part."

There's not a doubt in my mind that Americans are allergic to talking about their money. The financial-services industry is responsible for providing financial literacy to the general population—either one person at a time or in groups. Every face-to-face appointment is an opportunity to help a client or customer to be smarter with their money, to feel a sense of true financial security, and to plan for their future in a more comprehensive, intelligent manner. If you can convince someone to sit with you and talk about their finances, you are more than 80 percent of the way to getting them to those goals.

The "selling" part is *never* the hard part. Getting in the door is.

Getting in front of people, when they know you're going to talk to them about their money, has always been, and will remain, the hardest part of this profession.

Most of the companies I've worked with have spent too little time on marketing and phoning skills. It's amazing anyone survives his or her first three years in this business.

I have completely redesigned my former *Scripts* & *Tips* book to reflect changes in our society. *We have to change* the way in which we market and approach new prospects. Despite some companies' clinging to their past, I will unequivocally say that *dialing for dollars is dead.* If you require your advisors to dial a certain number of times, or for a certain number of hours per week, you are living in another century—and I don't mean the twenty-second century or beyond. Moreover, you're crippling your team. There's no amount of dialing that will result in enough appointments per week for any advisor.

Some Facts: In 1992 I began keeping phone statistics for the financial-services industry. The contact rate (i.e. dials to pick-ups) back then was 45 percent. For the rest of that decade, the contact rate dropped to 36 percent and then ended the century at the 30 percent mark. As we moved into the 2000's, we struggled to stay at 30 percent. Today, the contact rate is a mere 7 percent in most places, and it rarely rises above 17 percent for those who still keep track. These are unworkable numbers and should convince you things have changed.

You simply cannot randomly dial enough people to schedule the standard 8-10 new appointments per week.

This book shows you a new way to do things with much more success. For managers, it might be hard to teach these ideas if your career started—and grew—in a time when the phone was king. But now it's a smartphone and no one is picking up.

A word of caution: Years ago, using the phone was a good way to say hello and introduce yourself to a new prospect. That doesn't work anymore. Most people do not pick up their phone unless they already know who you are and what you do, and that usually requires already being a contact in their phone that they can recognize by caller ID when you call them. (Telemarketing, robocalls and overall annoyances have trained almost *everyone* not to pick up unless you know the person.) This reality changes scripting. Rarely do you have to introduce yourself since your call is often expected (i.e. you scheduled a **Phone Date)** and your information popped up (i.e. you're a **Contact**). My own outbound calls start with my prospect saying "Hi, Gail" after they pick up. Your outbound calls are probably answered in similar fashion.

This brave new world required an overhaul of my previous book. I believe I am continuing my service to an industry I admire and care about by telling you what's required today. What I taught seven, ten, twenty years ago was honest for that time.

This book is the right version for now.

A Word about Compliance

The financial-services industry is highly regulated regarding appropriate scripts and what you can, and cannot, say on the phone. Many of the scripts I've included here have been approved by most of the insurance companies I work for, but I include the following disclaimers:

I do not present this book as totally compliant with the rules of any particular insurance company.

Any agent using this book as a guideline must get approval from his/her own compliance department and/or manager prior to using any of the scripts or answers to questions and problems.

OUR NO PICK-UP CULTURE

THERE ARE SEVERAL REALITIES WE ALL NEED TO ACKNOWLEDGE. One, most people own a smartphone. Two, most people use that device only 7 percent of the time *as a telephone*. Three, many people don't listen to their voicemails. Four, some people don't even bother to set up the voice mail system on their smartphones. And lastly, we need to acknowledge the generational communication differences. Knowing your client's preferred method of communication (text, email, or phone) is as important as the names of their children.

For Experienced Advisors: If you believe all of these truths as, well, true, then you should have already changed your behavior when it came to prospecting and appointment setting from what the industry has done for decades. If you haven't changed what you've been doing, I'm glad you're reading this book.

For New Advisors: By reading this book, you'll start off in your practice doing what is appropriate for today's world.

Your marketing plan should constantly balance three elements: **The Digital** (i.e. texting and emailing), **The Vocal** (i.e. using the phone), and, most importantly, **The Personal** (face-to-face). All three work in concert. There is no formula for how much of each of them to do, but face-to-face marketing needs to be the biggest portion of your plan. In the past, phoning was a high percentage of your appointment-setting methodology. That is no longer true.

It is virtually impossible to create a week's worth of appointments by just sitting at your desk and making phone calls. I'll say this again: *dialing for dollars is dead*. Because the contact rate by phone has dropped to such a low number, there aren't enough hours in the week to dial your way to ten (or even eight) confirmed appointments. If you are starting a new practice, you've probably been told you need to schedule a certain number of initial appointments. But if you think you can sit and merely dial people to get all of your opening appointments, you'll be very disappointed. And frustrated.

You need a marketing plan that *puts you in front of people*. Constantly. This book will address face-to-face conversations because your ability to talk to new people in an effective manner is critical. You also need to work on a varied marketing plan to include different types of personal events to find the right fit. You should also develop a target market as soon as possible. Working one targeted group (e.g. architects, teachers, beauty shop owners, whatever) will help you to learn their financial challenges and become a friend of their industry, as well as, hopefully, well-known and liked.

TWO NEW IDEAS

PLEASE CONSIDER TWO NEW PROSPECTING BEHAVIORS. The first is to set **Phone Dates.** For decades, the financial-services industry has been relying on what I refer to as "random dialing"—i.e. you make an outbound call at your convenience. However, most people don't pick up a call unless they see a name *and* a number, which is why random dialing has lost its power.

Mathematically, as I explained in the Introduction, there is no way to reach enough people to fill your week by random dialing. You have to consider the current truths of people's phone behavior. Therefore, your first adjustment to this reality is to schedule **Phone Dates.**

A **Phone Date** is a mutually agreed-upon time to call another person (i.e. your prospect). The goal of this brief call is to schedule a face-to-face appointment. You will get 100 percent pick-ups if you schedule and confirm **Phone Dates.** They are expected phone calls.

You use the digital world—either texting or emailing—to ask the prospect for a time that works for them to speak to you briefly. The content of this request is about two sentences. The first sentence is always unique to that person and your relationship with them. The second sentence *must* be:

"SEND ME SOME TIMES YOU'RE AVAILABLE IN THE NEXT TWO WEEKS FOR A BRIEF PHONE CALL."

That's it. Don't change it. Don't make it a question either! An example of a **Phone Date** request could be:

> **"John:**
>
> **"It was great meeting you at the soccer game. I enjoyed our conversation and would like to continue it. Send me some times you're available in the next two weeks for a brief phone call."**

Of course, I would encourage you to try and schedule an appointment when you're with John, but that opportunity doesn't always come up. We will address how to transition a conversation so that it's appropriate to ask for a coffee appointment in person.

Once you get in the habit of scheduling **Phone Dates**, you'll find that the outcome of those calls is often an appointment. A **Phone Date** gets scheduled because the other person already knows you and is aware of what you do. Therefore, **Phone Dates** turn into appointments a lot more than random calls do, even random calls made in the past.

Here's a critical cultural shift for all salespeople to acknowledge: You do not introduce yourself on the phone anymore. You use other methods for getting known so that the prospect agrees to a scheduled phone call.

Years ago, we calculated the requisite dialing hours to reach enough people; then we used statistics to consider the contact-to-appointment conversion. Now you need to know how many **Phone**

Dates your appointment goals require. If you're no longer random dialing, how many **Phone Dates** do you need?

Here are some examples: If you need 10 new, confirmed appointments per week and would like to schedule 12 (since one or two will reschedule), then you need 14 **Phone Dates** a week. If you need 8 confirmed appointments per week, you'll probably schedule 10 unconfirmed appointments, so you need 12 **Phone Dates** a week. This means you would be making 12 dials a week to people who are expecting your call.

That is a big change from sitting and dialing for four to six hours per week. Even with your natural market, use a digital method (text or email) to ask your friends and family for a good time to talk since you're calling for a professional reason. Otherwise, a random call to a friend might be difficult to turn into a professional call.

Keep in mind that any appointment *set in person* will reduce your required **Phone Dates** for that week. Today's objective is to schedule more appointments in person than through the phone. We will talk extensively about how to do this in another chapter.

The second new idea is to recognize that you need to **Become a Contact** in other people's phones. Most folks ignore calls that only show a phone number, so this second new behavior is important to insure your calls get picked up.

Your first task is to create a **Digital Business** card in your own phone. Essentially, it's a contact of yourself, with specific fields filled in. Your second task is to practice texting your contact (i.e. your digital business card) to another person. You cannot be fumbling with your phone once you've met someone with whom you want to keep in touch. Sharing your digital business card must go smoothly.

Your contact in your own phone should follow the following sequence:

1. Open up a new contact in your phone.
2. Insert the proper information in the following fields:

   Your First Name

   Your Last Name

   Your "searchable" title (i.e. you need the word "financial" on this line, not your company name unless "financial" is part of it) **

   Your office phone

   Your cell phone

   Your business email (not your personal gmail or yahoo email)

   In the address section:

   First line: your Company name (not after your last name above)

   Second line: Street address

   Third line: City

   Fourth Line: State, Zip Code

   Social Media: copy the whole URL for yourself on LinkedIn

   Social Media: Put your URL page from your agency website or your own website

   **An alternative to putting your company name in the address section is to insert another line under your last name and have "financial advisor" first, then your company name underneath.

3. Take a good picture of yourself and insert it. Take as many photos as needed until you get one you like and in which you are smiling.
4. Save this information.

Now you have a professional **Digital Business Card.** Do not use your paper cards anymore. They get thrown away, stuffed in desk drawers and are not useful to your prospecting goals. Your task is to *get into people's phone* before they get away from you. *If you ever want to speak to someone again, you need to be in their phone.*

Practice sending it to people at least a dozen times. It needs to be second nature.

The combination of **Becoming a Contact** and scheduling **Phone Dates** will increase the number of people you speak to per week. And it decreases your dialing time significantly. You might be dialing only ten times or fewer per week. That's hard to fathom if your training was all about dialing hours, contacts made, etc. In our current culture, it is more appropriate to make **Phone Dates.** Without being a known person in someone's phone, you're perceived as a possible robo call. Good luck with that.

Getting "Ghosted"

It is possible to get "ghosted" by someone with whom you request a **Phone Date**. A nonresponsive prospect drives all of us batty. What you need to do is begin controlling your reaction to these non-responders by remembering that people have lives that don't include your goals. Try them again in a couple of days. Keep track of everyone you think to ask for a **Phone Date** since things change. Don't become a pest by texting or calling them constantly.

THE STRUCTURE OF A PHONE SCRIPT

THE SCRIPTS IN THIS BOOK ARE OFFERED WITH THE ASSUMPTION THAT YOU ARE only setting an **initial appointment with either a new prospect or a new appointment with an existing client.**

The biggest phone mistake is using language that assumes you are already someone's financial advisor. *It is during the initial appointment that you and the prospect actually decide whether or not you are going to have a business relationship.* If your words on the phone sound assumptive, you will not get the appointment.

Here's an example: Never put the words "help" and "you" next to each other in a sentence. Once you say those two words together, you've placed yourself in the role of advisor. That role has not been granted you. "I can help you to manage your retirement money." "I can help you to develop a better benefit package for your employees." These sentences make you their advisor. If the first appointment hasn't even happened, how could that be?

The second biggest mistake I hear agents making is providing solutions to a person based on a guess of what their financial issues might be. Being a professional gives you a ton of knowledge about how people need to manage their money and overall financial life.

When you meet new people and acquire even basic information about them, your brain just starts churning out ideas for that person. This is a crime I call "leading with solutions." The problem with doing this is that you have not been picked as their advisor, so why do you think they're interested in hearing your ideas about their money? It's hard to turn off what you know, but I'm asking you to keep your ideas to yourself. That type of scripting is just dead wrong.

If you've had a face-to-face encounter (like at a social event or a networking event), and you scheduled a **Phone Date**, you might have "advanced" the relationship to where the prospect is already interested in visiting with you. In that case, do not overscript the call!! You might not need to say more than, "Hi, it's Gail. We met at John's barbeque last week and agreed we'd get together for coffee to talk more about your business. I have my calendar open, so what's better for you, this week or next?" *And then shut up!!* If you've done the work of getting someone to agree to meet with you in another venue, then just use the phone to set the appointment. There is no convincing required! (More on this later.)

All appointment-setting scripts have a structure. All scripts have the same seven components: A through G, each of which is defined in the next paragraph. Most of the time, you need one of each. But certain situations will call for a shorter script. The challenge is to say as little as is needed to get the face-to-face appointment. Too often we talk too much, and it is perceived as babbling. Or you're trying to convince someone to do something. Neither strategy is effective.

Here is a quick glance at each component:

A: Your Greeting
B: Introducing yourself (with people who have your digital business card, this will not be necessary)
C: Your Company (again, this might not be necessary)
D: Your Relationship to the prospect *plus* your motivation for the call
E: Your Offering (first time you mention the appointment)
F: The Benefit of the appointment
G: The Close: asking for the appointment

There are three D categories, based on how you obtained the prospect. D1's are the easiest; D2's are next, and D3's are the hardest.

After you say "Hello" to someone you've met in person and exchanged digital business cards, they know who you are, in which case you will probably move directly into the D component.

D1: This group is called **Memory Jog** leads. Anyone who knows you or has met you falls into this category—i.e. friends and family, people with whom you share hobbies, vendors you use, alumni groups to which you belong, former co-workers or clients, current clients, seminar attendees, people you meet at expos/fairs/shows, canvassed leads, your neighbors, people you meet at social or networking events, charities, political groups, civic or volunteer groups in which you're active, and people you accidentally meet while doing whatever it is you do around your community (i.e. all the folks you know through your children's activities). In essence, anyone who has met you in person and knows you at least somewhat.

D2 leads are people who you've been **told to call by someone else**. The best type of D2 lead is an introduction to a referral. The other people you are "told to call" could be leads provided by your company (orphan policy holders, another agent's "neglected" clients, associations for which you/your company provides their benefits).

D3 leads are the hardest because you have no relationship with them. The four types of leads in this group are **direct-mail recipients** and any **responders** to a direct-mail campaign; **purchased leads** (from a company that sells them to you because the prospect is interested in a specific product or idea); **internet leads** (when you sign up to receive requests for quotes on products via various internet sites); and **cold calls**. It's harder to write a script for D3's because you have to eliminate the relationship part of the sentence. There aren't any D3 scripts in this book because my goal is to eliminate the need for this type of prospecting in your practice.

E—**Your Offering**. This is where you mention the idea of getting together with the prospect. It is just one sentence and is created from three parts: The first part is a verb that **invites** the other person to be with you; the second part is the verb of **what you will do** when you are together; and the last part is a noun describing **what you will talk about**. It can be drawn like this:

Invitation verb + Action verb + Noun

For example:

"I'd like to get together to share with you the total scope of the work that I do."

Or, *"I'd like to meet with you to discuss some of the ideas that Jason thought were interesting."*

F—The Benefit of the appointment for the client. The tricky part of writing a benefit is that you have to remember it is the positive emotional outcome of the appointment for the prospect. You are not selling a product; rather, you are proposing a new relationship to this person. A possible benefit (the underlined part) following the E example above would be:

"I'd like to get together to share with you the total scope of the work that I do. That way, you can use me and all the resources of my company, in any way that makes you feel the most comfortable."

G—The Request for the appointment—i.e. **the close**. You use an alternative choice close, but you must use an updated version. Here's the old way: "Which is better for you, Monday at 3:00 or Wednesday at 4:00?" To update your language, use larger concepts of time. Or you can offer two places to meet. Here are three examples:

"What is the least hectic time for you, earlier or later in the week?"
"In general, is earlier or later in the day easier for you?"
"I'm happy to drive to your home, or if you prefer, we can meet at my office."

Do not ask yes or no questions at the end. Words such as "Does that sound interesting to you?" are deadly!

Here's an interesting psychological fact: Most people, when offered two choices, will pick the second choice *more than 50 percent of the time*. Note the order in which I did the "Where do we meet?" close. That is also the reason I don't recommend sticking with "Which is easier for you—days or evenings?" It's better to say, "Which is easier for you—earlier or later in the day?"

Here is an example of a complete script, by an experienced advisor to their natural market:

> **"Hi, this is Gail and I'm calling for two reasons. (A & B) * How are you handling Jessica being away at college? (Let this part go for a minute or two.)**
>
> **"You know that I've been in financial services for over 10 years, and in all that time I've never called you on a professional basis. I'd like to rectify that with this phone call and position myself as an additional financial resource to you and your family. (D) We can set a time for me to visit with you and Bob, and I can show you the total scope of the work that I do. (E) That way, you can use me, and all the resources I have at my disposal, in any way that makes you feel the most comfortable. (F) I know that even with your youngest away at college you are still very busy, so what is the least hectic time for you generally—earlier or later in the week? (G)"**
>
> * This would be a person you know, so your company name would not be included.

An alternative to this script over the phone is the **Apology Script**, which is best done in person. It uses a lot of this language, but it has more impact because you are face to face.

Most of the scripts in this book come with an explanation if they don't completely follow this format. If you meet more people in person, your phone calls and scripts will be very short and have fewer of the components. Each situation is fully described so that you understand why a script is written so briefly. Other phone calls require a full ABCDEFG format.

Some marketing events can have more than one potential outcome. The next chapter will help you to know how much to say since too many words are just as bad as not enough words. And, as always, your choice of words is critical.

How to Not Sound Canned

If you sound like you are reading your script, then you will defeat the purpose of having a well-written script. The best way to sound natural, but prepared, is to write a script, making sure you have all the necessary components discussed in "The Structure of an Effective Script." Then read it, *out loud.* After feeling more comfortable with the words, you need to rewrite the script in bulleted phrases. That way, you will "talk" the key points in the proper order and remember the important words.

This will help you to use your natural gift of talking, but it will also keep you on track with what you are trying to say. Using a sample script, I show how it is in the book, and how it should be reverted to your "cheat sheet" when you are on the phone:

"Hi, it's ________________ I wanted to let you know that I started a career as (an agent, financial advisor) at (company), and I decided I am going to build my practice around the people I care about the most. In fact, they asked us to list those people and, of course, you were on the top of my list. I'd like to position myself as a financial resource to you and find a time when I can show you the new scope of the work that I do and then you can use me, and all the resources at my disposal, in any way that makes you feel the most comfortable."

FORMAT FOR ACTUAL CALLS

- Started a career
- Build my practice
- People I care about the most
- List those people
- Top of my list
- Position myself
- Financial resource
- Get together
- Share with you
- Scope of the work that I do
- Me, expertise, resources
- Any way that makes you feel the most comfortable
- Less hectic

Remember: Write a complete script first, *then* rewrite in abbreviated form.

MARKETING IDEAS AND SCRIPTS

FACE-TO-FACE MARKETING

IN A WORLD WHERE IGNORING YOUR RINGING TELEPHONE IS ACCEPTABLE BEHAVIOR, it becomes harder and harder to create a financial practice just sitting at your desk. Due to the unbearable low contact rate, it is impossible to produce enough appointments each week by merely dialing. Even a referral (i.e. a name and phone number from a client or COI [Center of Influence]) will not answer their phone if you are not a contact. A little later we will discuss different types of marketing activities and the best follow-up phone scripts.

When you are with someone in person, you might be able to suggest a follow-up coffee appointment. Your main goals are to get into the other person's phone (for any potential follow-up contact) and to steer the conversation where you want it to go. That is a key factor in any face-to-face conversation. Also, you want to get to know the other person first, instead of starting out by talking about yourself.

Even though face-to-face situations allow you a better chance at a coffee appointment, many advisors are not skilled at the art of conversing. There is a difference between being a good **social** conversationalist and knowing how to have a more productive **intentional** conversation.

Business Networking + Social Events

I admit it: I was trained in networking by a couple of experts. Although I love to talk to people, I did not come by it naturally. I can easily engage strangers in all kinds of situations, but to skillfully network—that's another story. I am grateful to my friends Andrea Nierenberg and Michael Goldberg for schooling me on how to be a good networker. I have embraced a lot of what they teach and have applied their philosophies to what I do.

In social situations, you need to know how to gracefully move the conversation to where you want it to go. At a networking event, your business intent is embraced and encouraged. Knowing the difference between these will help you to choose the right sequence of questions to ask. You need to be more subtle in a social situation, and you're *less likely* to attain a coffee appointment. Many networking groups, such as your local Chamber, will encourage people to continue to grow relationships through one-on-one meetings after the group-endorsed event. Asking for a follow-up meeting is appropriate.

In any of these face-to-face initial conversations, your primary goal is to figure out who the other person is. If you're inherently curious about other people, you'll excel at this. You might already be a great listener and can easily get others to talk.

The curious part needs to be more prominent than the profiling part. Again, using Michael Goldberg's questions on pages 20-21 will help you to see how you can get into a deep discussion about someone's work life. But if it is not done in a natural, curious way, any sequence of questions will feel more like an interrogation.

Here are the first rules of being a good guest and a good networker:

Never use your elevator speech other than in an elevator.

I am sure many of you think the above is blasphemy, but **it's important to deflect off of yourself** when asked, "What do you do?" and smoothly get the other person to talk first. If the other person greets you with a quick "What do you do?" the best answer to is to say, "I'm boring, let's talk about you. Tell me what you do when you're not balancing your food on your lap." Or you can say, "I'm boring. I'm a consultant. Tell me about yourself." And start asking questions. It works. Every time I've done this in a social situation, I've never been "caught" not answering the question.

Never talk about yourself first.

Your goal is to get the other person to talk about himself or herself as much as possible so you can start to frame how you will introduce your career. I strongly suggest you practice what I'm suggesting in this section. Get out and talk to people, and get them to tell you about their work life for no less than ten to fifteen minutes. Don't try to set an appointment. Just practice doing these types of conversations. The suggested questions are not a checklist—they are suggestions. Perceiving these questions as "I must ask all of these in this sequence" will make you seem like the CIA. The sequence of these questions might, or might not, work. It depends on where the conversation goes. You want to avoid going off on tangents, but keep the conversation natural.

Questions to Ask at a Networking (Business) Event*:

- Have you been to this event before?
- What keeps you coming back?
- How did you learn of this event?
- What type of work do you do?
- Do you like what you do?
- How did you get involved in that field?
- What made you change your career path?
- What are your goals for the year?
- What are your long-range business goals?
- Do you have personal goals you're looking to accomplish?
- What are some personal goals that you've failed to accomplish in the past?
- How do you market your business?
- How do you get most of your business?
- Are there other events you attend?
- Do you have a target market?
- Who is a perfect prospect for you?
- Who are the best referral sources for you?
- Who are you looking to meet here?
- How can I help?

Questions to Ask at a Social Event*:

- How do you know (host's name)? (Allow this part of the conversation to continue.)
- When you're not balancing food and a drink, what do you do?
- Do you like what you do?
- How did you start your business?
- How is business going?
- Were you (or your industry) affected by the recession?
- Why do you think your business survived?
- Who are your best clients?
- How do you market your business?
- How do you get most of your business?
- How many employees do you have?
- Are you looking to grow your business (or are you looking to retire)?
- What's the hardest part of your business/industry?
- Where is your business heading in the next few years?
- How can I help you?

*Michael Goldberg—knockoutnetworking.com

Most conversations start with whatever you are sharing—the event, the venue, the weather. That's always good to keep in mind because it gets people relaxed(see the section on Trade Shows). You then can move to talking more specifically about them.

If you're not a natural talker, you might find this a bit challenging at first. But keep practicing. You need to learn to have "no goal" conversations. Go to Starbucks and talk to people. Go to more MeetUp events and talk to people. Practice on people you see regularly (your dry cleaner, other parents at the school pickup line) but haven't really spoken to in depth. Even while practicing, you will be stunned at how much people like to talk about themselves when there is a good listener encouraging them.

The goal is to get enough information about their life so that when they stop talking and then ask you, "So what do you do?" (because they realize they've done all the talking), you'll be able to construct a unique answer to the question. Your description of your work will always be something that relates to their story. **You will wrap your practice around what they told you about themselves.**

Now you can see why an elevator speech doesn't work. Every conversation requires you to describe what you do in the context of the person you are with. There's no *one* answer.

How do you stop the conversation? Your goal is to choose something they've shared that you can use to describe your practice. But you don't stop at that issue, you keep them talking. Once you have sufficient information about them, allow a "pregnant pause" in the conversation. (Drinking something or taking a bite of food will create that pause.) They will immediately recognize they've done all the talking and turn the conversation on you. Their next question will often be "So what do *you* do?"

You have to **create a unique answer each time**. But they all start with five important words:

"You know when you said . . . "

You choose something from the conversation about their life and then relate your financial practice to that. Obviously, when you are asking the questions, you really need to be listening to their answers and filing away one or two in your head. You might find that someone gives you more than one thing to "latch" onto, but you need to **pick one** for your answer on which to follow up on. "So what do you do?" is followed by "You know when you said," with a repeat of something they said (nearly exactly) and then add, "I work with people in that exact situation. " Or "I've had clients who were having that exact challenge and we worked through it." Here are some examples:

Example: "You know when you said you don't know how you will exit your business? I just worked with a client on that challenge."

Example: "You know when you said that in your industry you're constantly fighting for talent? I have a few clients who have that exact same issue."

Example: "You know when you said you can't figure out how to balance saving for your retirement and helping your children with their tuition? I have a lot of clients in that same boat."

Once you are talking about your career in the context of *their* lives, you become an interesting person. There has never been an interesting elevator speech written for the financial-services industry that works at a cocktail party or networking event. (If your management team is telling you to "go out there and tell everyone what you do," please give them a copy of this book.)

Describing your career and your professional skills this way will give you a better chance to create another meeting. Here on the next page is your next line:

"I'd like to continue this conversation, but in a more private place. Why don't we get together for coffee sometime next week?"

Or,

"I'd like to continue our conversation, but in another venue. Let's get together for coffee next week."

Two things: You must exchange contacts with this person ASAP and pull up your calendar. ***Do not start educating the other person*** on the very problem they just shared. The coffee appointment is when you can discuss their issue in more detail.

Sometimes you cannot get the other person to agree to an appointment right then. They might need to speak to an assistant who also schedules them. In this case, you should schedule a **Phone Date** so their assistant will be ready to set the appointment on Monday morning.

This procedure is something you must develop and perfect. You cannot practice it enough. Once you start engaging other people in conversation about themselves, you'll see how easy it is. Everyone loves to talk about themselves to an interested listener. **Be that listener**. It is an important part of being a good advisor.

Follow-up Scenarios for Networking or Social Situations

Scenario #1: You met someone, had a good conversation, and exchanged contact information, but you did not get to the point of asking to continue the conversation in another venue. Your next move is to text or email them for a **Phone Date**.

"John, I enjoyed our conversation at Sam and Ellen's barbeque last weekend and wanted to continue it. Let me know some times you're available for a brief call in the next couple of weeks."

Once you have the **Phone Date** and it's confirmed, your script would be:

> **"Hi, John, (small talk about event at Sam and Ellen's). I noticed that when we were talking, you had said you were concerned about keeping your most valuable executives at your company without literally tying them to their chairs. I had mentioned that I've worked with other CEO's in the same situation and wanted to find a time to go for either coffee or lunch so I can expand on that with you. What's generally the easier for you, earlier or later in the week?"**

Scenario #2: You met someone, had a good conversation but didn't exchange information so you're not in their phone. No coffee appointment was set either. You might have to ask the host of the event (whether business or social) for this person's contact information. Then you email them to ask for a **Phone Date**. (That's if the host tells you they prefer emailing. If not, you can text the content.)

Email Subject Line: (Name of Event or Host's name)

> **"Hi, John, I enjoyed our conversation at Sam and Ellen's house on Saturday and wanted to continue our conversation. Send me some times you're available for a brief call in the next couple of weeks."**

Once you have a **Phone Date** set, you would say:

> **"Hi, John, (small talk about event at Sam and Ellen's). I noticed that when we were talking, you had said you were concerned about keeping your most valuable executives at your company. I had mentioned that I've worked with**

other CEO's in the same situation and wanted to find a time to go for either coffee or lunch so I can expand on that with you. What's generally easier for you, earlier or later in the week?"

Scenario #3: You've met someone in person, had a great conversation but were unable to get the coffee appointment. You scheduled a **Phone Date** to call them. Your name will come up on their phone if you're calling a cell phone. (If you're now calling a business number, you may need to reintroduce yourself.)

"Hi, John, it's Gail. (small talk about the event where you met—keep under two minutes). I'm looking at my calendar for next week. What's a good day for us to meet for coffee—or lunch if you prefer?"

Keep it super short. Do not go into more about what you do as an advisor. This is not the place to do that. You don't want to lose the reason for the coffee appointment by getting too enthusiastic on the phone and giving away all your ideas.

YOUR NATURAL MARKET

Whether you are a brand-new advisor or have years of experience, calling the people you know can be tricky. Let's acknowledge that there are three intimidating factors that inhibit your ability, or willingness, to call your friends and family:

1. The relationship is extremely close and more valuable to you than any one appointment. You can't risk messing up this relationship.
2. The person you are calling is one (or two) generations older than you.
3. The person is extremely rich, and our profession is about handling other people's money.

All of these are very real and can make you hesitate to call. That's normal. There is no such thing as "call reluctance." There are only people who don't have the right script for the situation.

There are five categories for dividing up your natural market list. I don't care if it's 50 or 250 people—every person needs to be assigned to a group.

Let's go through the **Five Categories of Your Natural Market**:

1. The very closest people in your world. That would be your parents, grandparents, siblings, closest friends, and family members you see and speak to often. It is *not* the cousins you see only at weddings and funerals.
2. This is the largest group and your next level of friends/acquaintances: the vendors you use (your dry cleaner, mechanic, hair dresser, favorite restaurant owners); neighbors; buddies you play any sport with; people you meet at clubs and organizations; your children's friend's parents. These folks are not the closest in your life (who are your Number 1's) but they know you, and you spend some time with them.

3. Anyone you haven't seen for more than a year. That would include former college professors, former co-workers, extended-family members, former classmates.
4. People who would be more valuable to you as a Center of Influence (COI) than as a client. That would include important people in your community, someone who might be "the unelected mayor of your town," or a professional person such as an accountant with whom you might be able to cross-refer clients.
5. Anyone who is in your world and ridiculously rich. If they are a generation older, that's more intimidating. (Such as your best childhood friend's father or your super-rich uncle.)

Each of these groups has their own scripts. You cannot possibly use the same script on a professor you haven't seen in three years and your closest friend on the planet.

Dealing with "How are you?"

Prior to sharing the suggested scripts, we need to take a detour to the treacherous question, "How are you?" With natural market calling, it is very easy to get caught up in a long-winded conversation. To get control of this, you need to change your opening statement. Or you might get taken down a rabbit hole of personal updates.

Instead of opening a conversation with "Hi, Janet, how are you?" I am going to suggest a different opening. ***You must practice and memorize it.*** Your old habits will kick in if you don't work at changing your opening line. Please write this down and put it in front of where you make your calls:

> **"Hi, _______________, it's (your name) and I'm calling for two reasons."**

Now you have given the listener a heads-up that this phone call is *not* just a regular friendly one. Next, you will insert a specific question about that person's life (e.g. "First, I wanted to know, how is your house painting going?" or "First, I wanted to ask—did you have fun at your niece's wedding?") **If you cannot compose a highly specific question about someone's life, then you don't know them well enough to ask, "How are you?"**

Allow a minute or two for the question to be answered. To start the rest of the script, say:

"The other reason for my call . . . "

And continue talking.

You will be shocked at how much this will limit the personal stories. You've opened up the call by declaring there are *two agendas.* They will **reduce** their "How are you?" answer because of this. I have challenged many of my advisors to try this technique. They are always surprised that it works. You do not need to have a ten-minute conversation with people you know before transitioning over to your professional agenda. And, keep in mind, it is now common to get interrupted by call-waiting, and suddenly your friend says, "I gotta go!" and you've lost the whole call.

Stop using "Is this a good time to talk?"

Here is another new phrase you need to memorize:

"I know you're busy, so I'll be brief."

Instead of using the outdated "Is this a good time to talk?" you should be using the above line. "Is this a good time to talk?" is a product of random dialing, not someone who schedules **Phone Dates**. If we have scheduled a call at 10 A.M. on Tuesday, and you call me at 10 on Tuesday, I clearly have made the time. So don't ask if it's still a good time.

If you call a relative or friend at work, they will probably pick up because they know it's you. Use the above instead of "Is this a good time to talk?" and don't ask "How are you?"

An alternative is to simply state, "I'm calling you at work and from my own work desk because this is a professional call."

These subtle updated changes are important. A lot of our conversations have old habits attached to them. "How are you?" and "Is this a good time to talk?" are two things that need to be reassessed. Make sure to be aware of your unconscious use of these two opening questions.

One last, new idea: Sometimes you should just take a stab at getting someone *now*. Send this text to a person you know if you're having trouble reaching them. Sometimes, it works. "I wanted to have a brief call with you. I'll call you in five minutes."

Scripts for Natural Market Groups

Group #1: For New Advisors

"Hi, this is ________ , and I'm sure that you've heard about my new career with (name of your company). I'm really excited about it and the reason I've called is that I would like to position myself—and my team*—as an additional financial resource to you. I'd like to set a time when we can get together so that I can share with you the total scope of the work that we do. That way, you can use my team, our expertise, and the resources of our company any way that makes you feel the most comfortable. With that in mind, what is less hectic—days or evenings?"

*(If you bring your manager with you on your appointments, using "my team" and the pronoun "we" is important.)

"I wanted to let you know that I started a career as (an agent, financial advisor) at (company), and I decided I am going to build my practice around the people I care about the most. In fact, they asked us to list those people and, of course, you were on the top of my list. I'd like to position myself as a financial resource to you and find a time when I can show you the new scope of the work that I do and then you can use me and all the resources at my disposal in any way that makes you feel the most comfortable."

"I don't know if you've heard, but I've become involved in a new career that I'm really excited about, and I wanted to call you to share my news. I've joined (company) and I'm focusing my work on helping the people I know best to address their financial goals. At this juncture, I simply would

like to position myself and my team as an additional financial resource to you and spend some time together to show you the total scope of the work that we do. That way, you can use me and all the resources we have in any way that makes the most sense to you."

Group #1: For Experienced Advisors

If you've been neglecting your natural market and have been a financial professional for more than two years, you should conduct an **Apology Tour.** This script is best done in person, but can be adapted to a phone call. **Do not change the word "rectify."** It is critical to the presentation.

"John, I'm so glad I bumped in to you because I need to tell you that I owe you an apology. (Pause and let them hear what you just said.) You know that I have been in financial services for more than _______ years, and in all that time, I've never reached out to you on a professional basis, and I need to rectify that. I would like to be an additional financial resource to you, and I want us to get together so that I can share with you the total scope of the work that I do. That way, you will be better able to use my expertise any way that makes you feel the most comfortable.

"I know you're usually very busy, but when can we go for coffee or lunch?"

If you're ready to call other members of your family and people you've never called, then you can use these following scripts as well:

"Hello, this is _______________. As you know, I have been in financial services for more than ________ years, and in all that time, I've never called you on a professional basis and I am rectifying that with this phone call. I would like to position myself as an additional financial resource to you, and I'm calling to set a time for us to get together so that I can share with you the total scope of the work that I do. That way, you will be better able to use my expertise any way that makes you feel the most comfortable. With that in mind, when would you like to meet—this week or next?"

"Hi, it's (your name). I'm calling you because I feel that I have been professionally irresponsible in that I have never called you and offered you my assistance in my professional capacity. I would like to position myself as an additional financial resource to you. In order for you to best figure out how to do that, I'd like to get together and share with you the total scope of the work that I do. That way, you'll be able to use my experience and knowledge any way you see fit. When can I take you out for a cup of coffee—this week or next?"

Group #2: Acquaintances, Friends, Vendors

"Hi, this is ________, and I'm sure that you've heard about my new career with (name of your company). I'm really excited about it, and the reason I've called is that I would like to position myself—and my team—as an additional financial resource to you. I'd like to set a time when we could

get together so that we* can share with you the total scope of the work that we do. That way, you can use me, my team, and the resources of our company any way that makes you feel the most comfortable. With that in mind, what is less hectic—days or evenings?"

(Change the pronouns back to "me" or "I" if you are experienced and don't work on a team)

Business Owners You Know

"The reason I'm calling is that I've made a career switch to (company), and I was in a business concepts class the other day and thought of you. They were discussing ideas that can save a small business owner like you important money, enough that it would affect your bottom line. I'd like to schedule an appointment to talk to you briefly about these ideas because if I were able to show you how to save money in your business, I'd certainly like to do that."

"Last week I was sitting with a client whose business is just like yours, and I thought of you. I wanted to give you a call because, in my financial practice, my primary focus has been on assisting business owners in enhancing their financial position. I'd like to get together and show you some of the ideas I shared with my other business client."

If you've called your natural market once and want a second shot, try this script:

"I was sitting in a class that was primarily about (small businesses, young families saving for college, whatever . . .),

and I kept thinking of you. I wanted to call and invite you to join me for a cup of coffee so that I can give you some of these really terrific ideas that I have learned. I felt that I would be neglecting you if didn't share them."

Sometimes, you **overhear a financial concern** when you're with your friends and family. If you can't take them aside to a private area, then you need to make a phone call at a later time. The language in this script works both in person and on the phone:

"Hi, this is__________. We recently were at (event), and I overheard you mentioning a concern about (example: paying for college, paying for benefits, the current economy). Because I am a financial professional, I hear those kinds of comments with a different ear, so the reason for my call today is to position myself as an additional financial resource. You may remember I am with (company), and I'd like to schedule a time when we can sit down and I can show you the total scope of the work that I do. Then you can decide how you might want to use me and all my resources."

"Hi, this is _____, and we were at (event), and during a discussion you said that you were concerned about ________. As a financial professional, I hear those kinds of comments with a different ear, so it motivated me to call you. I'd like to offer to position myself as an additional resource to you and your family/business and get together so I can show you the total scope of the work that I do. Then you can use me and all my resources any way that feels most comfortable to you."

If you've moved from a former financial company and now wish to call your former clients, you can use this language:

> **"Hi, this is ____________________ (from old company, if appropriate). I don't know if you've heard, but I have made a lateral move in my career, and I have partnered with a terrific organization, _________. I did this because I thought it would be good for me and good for you. I would like to get together with you to show you the new scope of the work that I now do, and I am sure that I will be a more effective financial resource to you in my new capacity."**

Group #3: People You Haven't Seen for More Than a Year

A really "sales-y" thing to do is call someone after more than a year of not seeing or speaking to them, and start talking about your career as a financial advisor. I think the right thing to do is to invite that person out for coffee or lunch and follow all the advice in the first section on social networking.

If you are thinking, "I've never been out for coffee or lunch with this person," then why are they on your list? Maybe you've been pressured to provide a specific number of names, but you will absolutely blow it with this person if you start the call by discussing your new career. It's important to find out what's been going on with them prior to talking about yourself. Schedule lunch or coffee and use the techniques I've discussed.

Let me say this again, because it needs to take hold with you: going around handing out business cards and telling people what you do is not good form. People have an incorrect perception of this industry to begin with, so why add to the problem? You always need to be in a conversation over which you have some control, in order to properly explain your career so people can understand what you do. And needless to say, carrying a paper business card has already been discussed and replaced with your digital business card.

Call this person for a catch-up appointment, but don't get caught on the phone telling them what's going on with you. Save it until you've gotten them in the right setting.

> **"Hi, it's ____________ and it's been a while! I'm calling to find a time to get together for lunch or coffee so we can catch up. I'd like to know what you've been doing (how your family is, etc.) and let you know what's been going on with me as well. What's easier for you—this week or next?"**

Group #4: People More Valuable as a COI

There will be some people on your natural market list who should be seen as Centers of Influence (COI) rather than clients. If someone is in a profession that has a natural synchronicity with yours (accountants, certain attorneys, etc.) then use the suggested script below instead of one that tries to make them a client.

Another great Center of Influence might be someone in your community who is highly connected. Many small towns have an Unelected Mayor—the person who knows everyone and their kids for generations. I would definitely use this script with them. Maybe someone in your family is a well-connected, well-regarded member of their community. You might re-categorize them after some thought.

Yes, you can make these folks clients and *then* ask for referrals. But the following script might be an easier approach if they have known you your whole life and fall into the intimidating group of a generation (or two) older than you.

> **"Hi, this is _____, and I'm calling you for help with my business. I don't know if you heard that I have joined (company) and I'm pretty excited about it. I know that you are very successful and I wanted to set a time when I can visit**

with you and show you our process to get your opinion on it. For the privilege of picking your brain, I'd like to buy you breakfast/lunch. And I know you're busy, so what is the least hectic day for you—earlier or later in the week?"

Group #5: Extremely Rich and Intimidating

I've met new advisors who have been pushed to call people in this category. Yes, you need to call them, but you also need to put them in the right group. These folks should be mentors and advisors *to you.* Asking an uncle, who remembers you as a little kid and can buy and sell the whole family, to consider you for managing his money sounds pretty intimidating to me. Why not ask him to help you? That is where your relationship is comfortable. For this person, I suggest using the same script that you would for Group #4. You will get a much better response *and* you can gain a valuable mentor. Keep in mind that as you are sharing your process with #4's or #5's, you are showing them your presentation. Some advisors have told me that these listeners start to lean forward and show tremendous interest in what you do. This approach is a better way to get help, honest feedback, and, *maybe* (yes, just maybe), a new prospect.

"Hi, this is ______, and I'm calling you for help with my business. I don't know if you heard that I have joined (company), and I'm pretty excited about it. I know that you are very successful, and I wanted to set a time when I can visit with you and show you our process to get your opinion on it. For the privilege of picking your brain, I'd like to buy you breakfast/lunch. And I know you're busy, so what is the least hectic day for you—earlier or later in the week?"

SEMINARS

Agency-Sponsored Seminars

Many agencies have taken the lead in providing seminars to the community. The biggest complaint I hear from managers is that the advisors do not seem to "fill the room" often enough. If your agency provides the seminar, your primary role will be to call clients and people you know to invite them. Your script must clearly state the benefit of their attendance.

The goal is to verbally make the idea of this seminar attractive to your client or family member. The more personal, the better.

> **"Hi, Aunt Betty. I'm calling for two reasons. First (ask a personal question that is specific to her life, not a general "How are you?" which can lead to a tangent). The other reason for my call is that my firm is sponsoring a really interesting workshop, and when I heard about it, I immediately thought of you. It's about (brief description), and I thought you and Uncle John would really want to hear this information. The event is on (date, time, day of the week), and since we are serving a light meal, they've asked us to get an accurate head count. I'd like to save two seats for you."**

Advisor Seminars

Sending out seminar invitations to a targeted group can bring you a lot of business. However, three scripts might be required. If you are mailing or emailing invitations and want to follow up on those, you need a script. After the event, if you haven't immediately set appointments with the attendees but have their contact information (and they have yours), you need a script. If someone says they are coming and then don't show up, you need a script.

Following are the three scripts for this type of marketing:

> **"I'm calling you to follow up on the invitation I sent about the workshop on (topic) on (date). I think you and (spouse) would find it very valuable. We will be bringing our retirement planning specialist to speak and a lot of information will be shared. Because we are serving a dinner, and we also want to keep the group to a size that allows for interactive conversation, we need an accurate head count. Can I reserve two seats for you and ________ on the evening of (date)?"**

Invitation Follow-up for Client Invitation:

> **"Hello, this is _______ with _________. I'm calling to follow up on an invitation I recently sent you. It was about our upcoming workshop on ________. Many of my clients have expressed a concern and interest in this topic, so I've decided to offer more information in a public arena. I think this topic is one that relates to *our* conversations. I'm keeping the seating limited so that we can allow for questions. How many seats would you like us to save for you?"**

After Seminar—Expressed Interest in an Appointment:

> **"Hello, this is ________. At our workshop on ________, you indicated that you were interested in a private consultation/appointment so we can personalize the information for you. I'd be happy to visit with you to do that. Where is the best place for us to meet—your home or my office?"**

Invited to Seminar—Didn't/Couldn't Attend:

> **"I am following up with those who were unable to attend our (title) workshop and offering to get together with you to discuss some of the highlights of the program. If we can schedule a time—either at your home or my office—I can give you a shortened version of the program and personalize it to your situation."**

Please be aware that all of these follow-up calls will be hampered if you don't get your information into the phones of the seminar attendees while they are there. There needs to be a point during the actual seminar when you instruct them to put the best phone number for your team into their phones. This will improve your follow-up contact rate dramatically.

TRADE SHOWS/FAIRS/EXPOS

It's always best to meet people in person, so finding appropriate trade shows and other events to attend will give you that opportunity. Your first key decision is choosing where to participate. There are lots of options in large cities. In smaller towns, you might find that local fairs are a great place to meet folks. In either case, consider who will be attracted to the show. Only pay for a booth after you have helpful information on the expected attendees and other possible vendors. That information will give you clues to the appropriateness of a specific event.

My first piece of advice is to make sure your booth is open and inviting. It is traditional to find a horizontal table, one chair, and a garbage can at your assigned location. First, move the table so it's perpendicular to the flow of traffic. That will create an open space for people to step into. Keep your tabletop choices to a minimum (e.g. don't clutter it with a lot of brochures.) My best advice: Always bring Hershey's kisses. They're irresistible and they can be a conversation starter. Scatter them on your table.

The goal of this event is to **talk to people.** It's not to gather a ton of names who won't respond when you call later (especially if you are dealing with the non-business market). Yes, there might be business people at your event, and if you have a raffle, you might have some luck calling them back. But your goal is conversations, not business card collection. If it were twenty years ago, I'd agree more about having a raffle, but in our no pick-up world, the after-event calling becomes a nightmare. You end up dialing hundreds of people who don't respond, when you should be walking away from the event with secured **Phone Dates** and appointments.

Again, use the networking techniques to get people to talk to you. Since most attendees "graze" past booths, I get asked, "How do you get people to stop at your booth?" It's easy. Make eye contact and say "Hi." Then follow up with a question *about the event you are sharing*—"How are you enjoying the conference?" Remember: Conversation rule #1: Engage people around what you share. Then, use the same types of questions you use at a networking event:

"Why are you here? Are you getting the information you hoped to get? Have you been to this before?" (*then*) "What kind of work do you do?"

For each type of show, you need to customize your questions, but they follow the same pattern. If you successfully conduct real conversations, you should be aiming for these goals:

a. An appointment *or* a **Phone Date** for trying to set an appointment

b. Exchange of digital business cards

Follow-up to Trade Shows

Assuming you did not have a raffle, your follow-up calls will match the above situations. These calls are similar to what happens at any networking event.

If you got an appointment from a conversation, give yourself a pat on the back. Your only job will be to confirm the appointment via text or email.

If you scheduled a **Phone Date,** then your calling script is very short. No one grants a phone date without having knowledge of what you do, so keep it simple.

Your name should come up on their phone because you exchanged information.

> **"Hi, John, it's Gail. (Small talk about the event where you met—keep it under two minutes). Let's continue the conversation we started at (event). I'm looking at my calendar for next week. What's a good day for us to meet for coffee—or lunch if you prefer?"**

If you've collected business cards but didn't get a chance to have a good conversation with all of them, you need a short re-introduction script. This assumes you get them on the phone, but be prepared to deal with a **Gatekeeper**. (See Gatekeeper Section).

> **"Hi, John, it's Gail Goodman. We met briefly at the (trade show) but didn't have enough time to really find out more about each other's business. I'd like to continue our conversation and wanted to find out what would be the best time for coffee. I'd be happy to meet you at the closest Starbucks, or, if your week is hectic, I can bring you some caffeine when you need it. Which one sounds better?"**

CANVASSING

Most advisors and managers are not adept at canvassing. The reason? Most professionals I meet have been in sales for a long time. Their "growing up" years coincide with the time when phoning was king. I learned sales when the phone was highly effective and was never taught how to canvass. *However*, I'd like to discuss a form of "canvassing" that is not traditional and could be easier to learn.

There are two ways to canvass. The first is the most commonly known. You schedule yourself on specific days for two hours of canvassing specific neighborhoods. You go in and out of businesses and say hello, talk about their business and try to get a second opportunity. I do not have a script for this type of canvassing. Hopefully, one of your colleagues has successfully done this type of canvassing and can teach you.

An easier idea is to add thirty to forty-five minutes to your **already scheduled appointments** and specifically use that time to meet your client's "business neighbors." Since you often see a client three or more times before your sale concludes, you are creating three or more reasons to say hello to the businesses next to them. For example: If your client has a dress shop in a strip mall, you can be sure she or he knows all the other store owners. If your client is an accounting firm in a corporate building, he or she knows the other suite owners on their floor. After conducting your normal business with your client, ask for permission to let these neighbors know you're their advisor. Then you use the excess time allotted to say "hello" to those new prospects. If you do this every time you see your clients (remember, this is *not* a one-call-close business) then you will slowly develop relationships with these business owners. They will know your face, your name, and why you keep visiting your client. By asking questions about *their* business, you will gain important information that will eventually give you a reason to suggest an appointment. Again, you are networking, not selling.

If you cannot figure out what to say to the neighbors of your clients, go back to the beginning of this section. You must be comfortable engaging any business person in a conversation. That is the essence of prospecting.

REFERRALS AND INTRODUCTIONS

Any business person will attest to the power of a referral. Getting endorsed by a happy client for the work you do, or a Center of Influence, is an important way to grow your practice. Our current challenge is that the acquisition of a name and a phone number is no longer adequate. **You need your referring person to help you get known by the new referral**. That is the best way to insure they will take your call.

Again, I am emphasizing that getting just a name and a phone number is inadequate. In the business world, an introductory email will go a long way in bypassing the Gatekeeper since that email will help you get a **Phone Date**.

This book is not about how to get referrals. Most advisors have been taught at least one technique for successfully getting a client to introduce you. Once that conversation has taken place, you need to ask for help in getting the referral to take your call. It's very easy to say:

> **"John, I appreciate that you are willing to introduce me to your close friend Adam. You also know that if I call Adam and I'm not in his phone as a contact, he probably won't pick up. I'd like you to send him my contact in a text, and just tell him three things. One: that you are my client, that I'm your advisor, and that you're happy with the work we've done. Two: please remind him to save the contact, and Three: to simply take my call."**

Here is an example of what you want your client to text:

> **"I'm extremely happy with my financial advisor, ____________. I've attached his contact information. Make sure you save it in your phone. I told him to call you. Take his call. It will be worth it."***

This can be modified to your personality but *do not* expand it. It should not be a speech. (It is assumed that you have your contact information in the phone of the referring person. If you have not done that, go back to "Face-to-Face Marketing.")

Once you know your client has sent the text, your next move is to request a **Phone Date.** If your client and the referral prefer texting, then ask for the **Phone Date** via text. Your request would be very short:

> **"I know that John has told you about me. I'm interested to hear your side of a couple of stories he shared. Send me some times you're available in the next two weeks for a brief phone call."**

> *All financial companies have rules about texting. In the above scenarios, the client is texting your contact information to the new referral. However, there are many companies that allow texting when it refers to the logistics of setting an appointment (such as the above).

Once you have secured a **Phone Date,** the vocal script will be:

> **"Hi, this is ______________. I know John texted you when we were together. I'd like to set a time to share with you the scope of the financial work that I do, and then you can see why he suggested that we meet. In general, what's the least hectic time for you—earlier or later in the day?"**

If emailing is the preferred method to get introduced, ask your client to use the following specific format:

The email is written *to:* The Client and *to*: You. The Subject line is: Introduction

The content of the email is a paragraph to the client about you, as well as a paragraph to you about the client. Here is an example of a good email introduction. (The assumption here is that John, your client, has composed and sent this.)

To: Adam Smith

To: Gail Goodman

Re: Introduction

Adam: Gail is my financial advisor and has done a terrific job for me. She's brought some intriguing concepts and ideas to my business and is super smart. I feel very comfortable with her, and I think you will, too. She is worth a conversation by phone, at the minimum. I highly recommend her.

Gail: Adam and I started our businesses at the same time. We are close friends and he knows my business well—and vice versa. I think he would be a good match for you since you are a straight shooter and helped me a lot. He will appreciate your directness and intelligence.

Enjoy,

John

Your next step is to hit **Reply All** and ask Adam for a **Phone Date**. John will see that you have followed up promptly.

Adam,

John speaks very highly of your business and the close relationship you've had since college. I look forward to hearing how you developed your business. Send me some times you are available in the next two weeks for a brief call.

Gail

Rule for Texting and Emailing: Never ask for an appointment digitally. Always be speaking to them, in your voice, in real time. Otherwise, you cannot deal with their reactions—especially the negative ones (the ones you call objections).

Referral Calls

If your referring person has either texted or emailed on your behalf, and you have a scheduled **Phone Date**, your call must be very short:

> **"Hi, this is ______________. Good to meet you on the phone and John speaks very highly of you. I'd like to schedule a time to share with you the total scope of the financial work that I do, and then you can see why (John) suggested that we meet. Generally, what's easier for you—earlier or later in the day?"**

If you **have not been able to get help from your client** (i.e. no text or email was sent, and you might not be in their phones), then you are going to have more trouble getting the new prospect on the phone. Here are some scripts if you magically get them to pick up:

> **"Hi, this is ______________, and a friend/ colleague of yours, (referring person), suggested that I give you a call. (Referring person) is not only a friend of mine, but she is also my client. I'm with (company), and we recently met and I did some very good financial work with (referring person) and she wanted me to call you. All I would like to do at this point is position myself as an additional financial**

resource to you and schedule a time when I can share with you the total scope of the work that I do. That way, you can use me in any way that makes you feel comfortable."

"Hi, this is ____, and a mutual friend suggested I give you a call. Harry Smith is both my friend and client, and I am his (agent, financial professional), and he speaks very highly of you. I am with (company) and recently, we met to discuss some ideas for ________, and he thought that some of the concepts I shared with him might interest you. What I'd like to do is get together, show you the total scope of the work I do, and then you can use me in any way that makes you most comfortable."

If a Center of Influence has introduced you:

"Hi, this is__________, and recently, I was with (referring person), and he suggested I give you a call. (Referring person) and I are friends, and we were talking about our businesses, and, as a financial professional with (company), he thought I could position myself as an additional financial resource to you/your business. I'd like to find a time when we can meet for a cup of coffee, and I can share with you the scope of the work that I do, which will allow you to figure out the best way to use both myself and all the resources of my company."

If You Have Been Referred to a Possible Center of Influence:

"Hello, this is __________, and I was referred to you by (referring person) and the reason I was calling is that I am looking for other professionals who can provide complementary services to my clients. I only give my clients Cadillac service and I am looking for other professionals who pride themselves on doing the same thing. (Referring person) thought you were that type of person and told me to call you. So I'm calling to see if I could set up a time for us to get together and discuss the possibility of pooling our resources for the benefit of our potential mutual clients."

Calling a Potential Center of Influence you know:

"Hi, this is ___________, and I'm calling because in my financial practice I am often in a position to need the services of an attorney/accountant, and I immediately thought of you. What I'd like to do is find a time when we can sit and talk in more detail about our respective practices and see if there is a basis for us to consider doing some referring to the other's clients."

Calling the Referral from a Center of Influence:
(Try to get your contact information sent in advance.)

"Hi, this is __________, and I was recently with ______, and he/she suggested that I give you a call. ________ and I are colleagues and frequently we find that our clients need the services of the other. That is the reason for my call. I am a financial advisor with (company) and I work with people on (financial issue that is appropriate for this client.) _______ suggested that we schedule a time to sit down, and I can share with you the scope of the work that I do and see how, along with (referring person,) I can be part of your professional team."

GATEKEEPERS

Important people have Gatekeepers. Over time, the number of Gatekeepers was severely reduced by the creation of voice mail. However, many business people still need someone to field their calls. Needless to say, you must be respectful and polite to this person. If you make their boss a client, a Gatekeeper can be very helpful to you during the sales process. I suggest you use my script when calling someone who is **not** a relative, referral, or friend. (I would also ask you why you are cold calling a business person, but I'll leave that argument for another book.) For those who know you, simply tell the Gatekeeper—"Tell him it's his friend, Gail Goodman." If you've been referred *and introduced*, you can tell the Gatekeeper—"Tell him that I am the person Harry Smith suggested he speak with."

> **"Hello, this is ______________________. Who am I speaking with?"**
>
> **(Get assistant's name)**
>
> **"______________ (assistant's name), you're in the best position to help me. I need to speak to ______________."**
> **(prospect)**
>
> **"Is he/she busy—you know, on the phone, in a meeting, or**
> (Speak this part slowly . . .)
> **can you please put me through right now?"**

Your goal is to get stopped if the prospect IS on the phone or in a meeting. You would not get to the last part (. . . put me through . . .) but immediately say:

> **"Should I wait on hold for a minute, or is there a better time to call when you'll be able to put me through?"**

Now you are engaging the Gatekeeper to help you. Always be prepared to be asked "What is this about?" Your answer has to have a benefit *to the Gatekeeper*, not the prospect.

Example: If you are calling someone with a Gatekeeper and you want to speak to the Boss (prospect) about virtually no cost benefits, you would say: "I'd like to speak to your boss about a program that allows you to keep your benefits, even if you change jobs."

Example: If you're calling the boss (prospect) about buy-sell agreements between the partners of the business, you might say: "I'm calling to speak to your boss about a way to keep the business going even if something happens to one of the partners."

See? The stated reason for the call to their boss has a good outcome for the Gatekeeper.

Association Endorsements

Many financial companies have helped their advisors create exclusive association alliances. There are tons of organizations that offer their members different kinds of benefits. Group insurance policies are popular. If you can become the association's "go to" person for these types of benefits, you will be introduced to a whole group of people who will immediately recognize you and be willing to talk to you.

The association needs to help facilitate your relationship to their members. It's often done through an announcement—sometimes a letter, sometimes an email, and often it's both. Once this introduction is completed, you can make calls to the members as the provider of their benefits.

Here is a script to the members of the association:

> **"Hello, Mr./Mrs. Business, this is (name) calling from (company). Our name is probably familiar to you because we have an alliance with (association) and are the approved provider for different benefits for the members. You have probably seen the letter from (association) announcing this relationship. I'd like to find a time when the two of us can sit down, and I will show you the scope of the work that we do for (association)'s members, and you can see how we're sharing creative ideas for their benefits program. What is the easier time for us to spend ( ) minutes—earlier or later in the day?"**

COMPANY LEADS

Orphan Calls

There is a variety of leads that I categorize as "company leads." You are asked to call these people because of their relationship with your company. The most common lead is the (poorly labeled) "orphan client." This is a policy holder who no longer has an advisor at the company, and you're asked to call this person to provide service, ideas, and answer questions.

I will immediately argue that the worst thing you can do is to call about a specific policy. The goal of an appointment with an orphan is to re-establish a working relationship with them, not to just "review" a single policy. You want to get a new fact find and provide a more comprehensive view of their finances. If you *only* bring up "a policy" (which might be the only item you see on their record), then your appointment will only be about *that* policy.

Agents have reported to me that it is very hard to initiate a comprehensive conversation about their finances when the premise of the appointment was a single policy. A new fact find and open conversation about their total financial life should be the goal. The suggested script has worked very well in getting the "orphan" to respond more positively over the phone. It is important to do this script with a smiling, happy, and friendly tone of voice. There is a pause after you ask if they want to hear the good news. Make your answer ("We have inherited each other!") highly dramatic and humorous. And then laugh—at least a little. Another human being will often laugh if you do.

Your goal is to make this person have a completely new reaction to you than to the other thirty or so advisors that previously called. Believe me, the client is more prepared for this call than you are! So be different; be funny and be sincere that you want to find out who they are and you're not there to sell them another policy.

If you *are* trying to sell them another policy, then my idea won't work for you. If you think there are some seriously good options with the current policy they own (e.g. they can get far more insurance now due to the morbidity rates dropping, etc.), then go for it. But if you want to create a new client and complete a new fact find, you have to go for a relationship-oriented script.

I stand by this one:

> **"Hi, this is _______ calling from the local office of (your company), and I'm calling with good news! (*Pause*) I'm pleased to tell you that we have inherited each other. (Laugh here.) The company has asked me to be your servicing agent, but right now you and I have a problem. You are a name on a manila folder (or computer screen) and I am a strange voice over the phone. I can't do business this way, so I'd like to buy you a cup of coffee so that we can both put a face to the name. What would be easier for you—meeting at a Starbucks, your home, or my office?"**

> **"I'm calling with great news! (*Pause*) We have inherited each other. (Laugh here.) However, you and I have a problem. Right now, you are a name on a manila folder and I am a strange voice over the phone. Since it makes me uncomfortable to service your account when I wouldn't even recognize you if we were to bump into each other at the grocery store, I'd like to schedule a time when we can get together—maybe for a cup of coffee—so we can both put a face to the name and be more comfortable with each other." (Close.)**

If you have a staff person making the calls for you, mostly the pronouns have been changed:

> **"Hi, (client), this is _______, and I work with (agent) at (company) in (town).**
>
> ***"I have good news! We have inherited each other.**** **(*Pause*). The company has asked (agent) to be your servicing agent and we would like to give you the best service possible, but right now we can't do that when you are just a name on a manila folder to us, and we are a strange voice over the phone to you. __________ would like to schedule a time when you can meet—maybe for a cup of coffee, so that you can both put a face to the name."**

Calling Your Mentor's C+D Clients

Many young advisors are asked to call some of the clients of a more experienced person or the clients of their own manager. It is common for the newer agent to be given access to the "C + D clients" of these more experienced people. They are expected to call these clients and re-establish the relationship by setting an appointment and doing a new fact find. This is a good thing.

However, when you call and reach the client, *do not say*, "I know it's been a while since (older agent) has called you . . . "

Really??? You've just announced to the client that your colleague is neglectful. I've heard hundreds of advisors make these calls with this opening line. Don't use it!

I've rewritten the beginning of the script to sound more professional.

Another language clue: You also cannot say, "I'm calling on behalf of . . . " because that is business-speak for "I'm his assistant." You are not an assistant. You are another licensed professional. Use the wording in my script so they recognize you are fully capable of meeting with them and discussing their financial life.

> **"Hello, this is (name) and I am (older agent's name)'s associate. You probably are aware that (older agent) isn't someone who makes unnecessary calls, but at this juncture, he's/she's asked me to call you. From time to time it makes sense to sit down with one of us and reassess some of the financial decisions you've made. One thing we know for certain is that things change—either your family situation or the market. I'd like to make sure that the programs you have in place are still working in line with your financial goals. I'm happy to drive to your house or you are always invited to visit our offices. Which is better for you?"**

If a staff person is calling your C + D clients, here is that version:

> **"Hi, this is ___________ from (associate's name) office. (Associate) asked me to give you a call and, as you know, he/she doesn't ask me to do that unless it's important. He/She feels that from time to time you should get together with him/her to reassess the financial decisions that were previously made because we know that for certain things change—such as the market and possibly your family situation. He'd/She'd like to get together with you in the privacy of our office. I'm scheduling next week, so what is the less hectic time for you—morning or afternoon?"**

Financial Literacy Programs

If the financial-services industry does not take responsibility for educating the American public about their money, who will? The medical profession is always out there telling us to get check-ups, mammograms, flu shots, etc. Why shouldn't the financial industry take on the challenge of educating the masses?

There are a number of ways you can get involved in financial literacy programs. Your company probably has some ideas for you. But, ultimately, you need to make calls to a variety of people in order to present this idea. In speaking with advisors and managers who are on this bandwagon, here are some ideas to try:

Community Group Outreach (Call the Executive Director):

> **"Hi, ____________, I've been reaching out to other (insert type of organizations) in (town) to offer a financial wellness program as a service to the community. It's an educational experience, with the goal of helping participants to have better control over their financial life. I'd like to find a time when you have 20–30 minutes so I can show you the curriculum that we've developed. Our research has found that financially educated people are happier and more productive, which is better for the overall community. What is less hectic for you—mornings or afternoons?"**

Referral:

> **"Hello ______, this is _________ with (company) here in (town). I was referred to you by ___________. He/She thinks very highly of you and your organization and recommended I reach out to you. Our firm conducted a financial literacy program for (referring person) and he/she thought we**

should share it with you as well. I'd like to find a time to sit down and share the details of the curriculum, which focuses on both individuals and families. In our research, we have found that the lack of financial literacy is wreaking havoc in America today. (Referrer) suggested we get together to see how it fits into your organization. I know you're very busy, but what is less hectic for you, mornings or afternoons?"

Business:

"Hi, this is __________, and I am with (company), and I am calling because our company is providing a free financial literacy program to local businesses. The seminar is designed for large (or small, whichever you're calling) companies who want to provide an educational benefit to their employees, and it's no cost to you. I would like to schedule a brief meeting to further show you the details of the program. Most employers would agree that financially educated and prepared employees means a happier, more productive workforce. In general, what is the less hectic time for you—before or after lunch?"

"I'm following up on an email I recently sent you regarding our corporate financial planning programs. I work with many benefits coordinators in providing a value-added service to your company, at no charge to you and with little work on your part. I'd like to set up a mutually convenient time when I can show you the benefits of having corporate-sponsored financial planning seminars for your employees. The win-win arrangement is that we do all the work and you get all the credit."

TARGET MARKETS

Having a target market makes your life easier. Most advisors realize they have "collected" a group of similar people within a couple of years into their practice. It's not crazy to recognize that we are all drawn to certain types of people. It is also common for your referrals to help create a "targeted" group since birds of a feather flock together.

My own journey toward having the financial-services industry as my target market followed the exact route described by those who professionally teach it. I had a couple of financial services trainers and managers agree to an appointment when I first called them, and then they referred me to other trainers and managers. I got invited to NAIFA meetings as a speaker, which launched my status as a "friend of the industry."

You need to know what the definition of a "target market" is before establishing one. It is a group of people who share something in common (either a profession or a recreational passion, or they have a reason to be considered a "group"); they have a means of communication; and they have meetings. For your practice, it's important they allow you to be part of their group. Some industries don't. (The AMA for one.)

If you want to start a target market, you can follow a series of steps that will ensure they are a viable group for you. There are several terrific books on target marketing, but here is the essence of it:

You need to make sure this is a good group for your services. The best way to do that is to interview people in the industry. Recently, I spoke to an advisor who was getting frantic from weeks of cold calling. In discussing the idea of a target market, he shared that his family has been in the building and construction industry for a long time. He had worked for nearly ten years with his dad, who owns such a company. That was his target market. In order to properly create this group as a target market, I suggested he follow a specific set of activities. You can do this as well. Let's assume you're interested in getting involved in the construction and building industry in your area.

The first step is to interview several owners of construction firms. Start with anyone you know in this business, and ask them for names and phone numbers of their professional colleagues. Create a list of appropriate questions to ask them so you can get a feel for the status of the industry, their issues, and concerns.

Each builder you interview can recommend others who are part of their local professional organization. Once you know five or six people in this market, you have established yourself as a professional who is interested in them. Remember to return to each person interviewed to share the information you acquired from their peers. (Everyone wants to know how others answered the questions, believe me.) This is part of establishing yourself as a professional who is useful and interested in them.

The next step is for you to reach out to the local organization of builders with the intent to join. If possible, call the Executive Director prior to joining, because that person will know more than everyone else about the industry trends, the group's concerns, etc. Because of the above activities, you will already know a few people.

At the meetings, incorporate the networking strategies discussed in this book. You don't ever want to appear as a "fox in a henhouse." Remember, you are still an "outsider." You need to be asking questions, listening, and learning. Volunteering to help will create more meaningful relationships with individuals on committees. Referrals should also start getting easier once you are a part of their clique.

Over time, a target market can become a critical part of your practice.

If you want to do research on a professional group and find their organization(s), here are two places that could help:

> https://en.wikipedia.org/wiki/List_of_industry_trade_groups_in_the_United_States

Or Amazon has a Kindle eBook for $0.99 with all associations listed:

https://www.amazon.com/Directory-Associations-Societies-Federations-Think-ebook/dp/B01945JGHE

In addition to choosing a group, researching members, and interviewing them, you want to have some ideas on how to "clone" them. Other than networking groups, the following is my favorite idea on how to create appointments with the folks you like the best.

Breakfast Meetings

My favorite idea on how to clone your best clients is through small breakfast meetings. Here's how they work: You plan a breakfast meeting for ten people at the best restaurant or hotel in your neighborhood. You pick four favorite clients who have something in common (they're all architects, manufacturers, independent consultants, retail store owners, whatever). You call those four clients and invite them to an exclusive breakfast meeting. When you call your clients, ask them to bring a professional friend similar to themselves, and it needs to be someone you do not know. Now your guest list is four clients, the four guests, yourself, and a guest speaker—*who is not you*. The speaker should be a Center of Influence of yours (or someone you want to create as a COI) who has a good twenty-minute speech that will be about something of interest to this group.

Example: Your favorite clients are female owners of small accounting firms. You invite four clients to come for breakfast (plan six names, just in case), and when they say yes, you ask them to bring another female accounting firm owner they know but you don't. Invite a Center of Influence who has something important to say to this group (e.g. a personnel specialist, an image consultant who works with professional women, a life balance coach, a specialty tax lawyer, whatever fits the occasion) and make sure they know there will be eight women who own their own firms. The content of the presentation *must* be of interest to your audience.

You have now bought breakfast for ten people—four great clients, the four "clones" of those clients, the speaker/COI, and yourself.

This is a win-win and something you can do once or twice a month.

Meeting new people can be challenging. Ask your clients to introduce you to people like them in a fun, interesting way. Cloning your favorite people is a great way to grow your practice.

Your Congregation

Many advisors are committed to working with their congregation—a group of people with whom you share something vital. And you see them regularly. You must be sure that "doing business" within the group is acceptable. The best way to get approval for approaching the other congregants (or the group as a whole) is to speak to the leader first. Here is a suggested script, but I would strongly suggest asking in person.

> **"I wanted to speak to you about setting up a time when we can discuss my helping our church/temple/congregation with an improved charitable giving program. There are several ways we can set it up so that the outcome is a clear win-win situation—there is more money for our congregation, but in addition there are tax benefits to the giver. These programs have been very successful in other churches/temples, and I'd like to see ours get the same increase in generous donations."**

Sample Target Market Language

Here are some examples of scripts for specific groups. The targeted group can be changed. They all require you to add a close at the end. Notice some of the language that can be incorporated, both on the phone and in person. Feel free to modify and use some of these for the groups you are pursuing:

> **"I specialize in working with florists since my family has been in the floral business for forty years, and I am familiar with the cyclical nature of the business. I have been able to sit down with other florists and assist in identifying appropriate concepts and ideas to meet their current or future goals."**

> **"As a former restaurant manager, I have focused my current work in the financial-services industry on helping my colleagues in the food business to be able to meet their financial goals. What I would like to do is visit with you and briefly discuss some of the financial programs that I think meet the unique needs of restaurant owners. In this short visit, we can get to know each other, and then if you think my ideas are helpful, we can take it from there."**

> **"Being a former manufacturer, I have focused my current work in the insurance and investment industry on providing ideas to executives in the garment center. These concepts are designed to help them handle their unique problems associated with cash flow, retirement, and other serious financial challenges. I would like to share some ideas that I think you will find helpful to achieve the financial success you deserve."**

"The last time we spoke, as you might recall, I was helping military families build a strong financial future. I am now working with (company) because it gives me the ability to be a financial resource to my friends who are in the service. I would love to sit down with you and (spouse) to show you the total scope of the work I'm doing, and then you can decide how to best use all of our resources."

BUSINESS MARKET

Retirement Specialist

Some advisors find they are great at working in the retirement arena. Specializing in retirement planning can be challenging, though. Managers in charge of company retirement plans are bombarded by calls. Some experienced advisors and managers will tell you to make two thousand phone calls as a way of becoming a specialist. *I would highly discourage this idea.* First, anyone who did this kind of calling before 2007 might have gotten somewhere before the first three hundred dials were completed. But in a defensive, no pick-up society, such as today's, this suggestion is disastrous.

The best way to start specializing in retirement planning is with the people you know. First, you want to approach any and all of your clients who are business owners. Maybe you forgot to bring up their retirement plan when you first met with them. Maybe you didn't feel you were qualified to talk about it at that time. But start by calling your existing business owner clients. Next on your list are your clients who are employed at companies that give them retirement benefits. They may be able to introduce you to the person in charge of their company retirement plan. Third, you should look to your natural market. Who is in business? Who works for a big company with a retirement package? Lastly, think of all the other people in your natural market who might have or need a plan—your doctor, dentist, pediatrician, landscaper, etc. Every one of these people has a relationship with you and will take your call.

If you're an experienced advisor, see the **Apology Tour** script (See Script Section) and adapt it to this scenario. One possible script for people you know is on the following page:

"Hi, __________________, it's me. I'm calling for two reasons. (Ask a personal question about their life and let this part of the conversation continue for a couple of minutes.) The other reason for my call is that I haven't spoken to you about the work my firm does for companies with retirement plans. I know you provide such a plan to your employees, and I'd be remiss if I didn't share with you some of the ideas that I've been sharing with business owners who are not my (friends/relatives). The unique approach we have is that we work from a service-oriented model. We analyze a variety of fees that can easily get expensive for the company. In addition, our goal is to protect the person with the fiduciary responsibility for the plan, making sure they are audit-ready at all times.

"I'd like to have a face-to-face meeting with you and the other executives who are in charge of your plan. What is less hectic for you—generally—earlier or later in the week?"

For Your Own Clients **:

"Hi, __________________, it's (name). I'm calling for two reasons. First, I wanted to briefly talk about (product, form, whatever reason you would call them—even a personal one). The other reason for my call is that I recently did some work with a client who has a retirement plan very similar to yours. I have been remiss in not telling you that I have access to a variety of resources to help you with your company plan as well. Without going into a lot of detail

right now, I'd like to schedule a meeting where I can describe the analysis we do on a variety of features of a retirement plan. I know your days are busy, so I'd be happy to schedule a time early in the morning before things get too hectic."

For Clients who Can Refer You Within Their Company: **

"Hi, ________________, it's (name). I'm calling for two reasons. First, I wanted to briefly talk about (product, form, whatever reason you would call them). The other reason for my call is that I know that at (their company) you are participating in the retirement plan. Our firm has an exclusive division that works with the people who are in charge of plans like yours. The way your retirement plan is managed can have an impact on your own portion of it. I would like to speak to the person in charge of your plan, but I would need you to introduce me to them."

** Remember, if you are already scheduling an appointment with this client, this entire script can, and should, be done in person.

Corporate Nesting

Once you obtain a client who is part of a big company, asking about their benefit plan is part of your initial fact find. Eventually, you should become very familiar with the benefits and what they can and cannot do for the employees. Then you're in a position to call other employees within that company. It's best if you can get direct referrals from your own client, of course, but you can also approach other employees on your own.

Here is a sample script for this type of calling:

> **"I do a lot of work with (their company) employees in helping them to assess their current benefits package, especially their retirement plan. Most plans only provide an 800 number for employees to get personalized information, or questions answered, and I would like to position myself as an additional financial resource to you as I've done with some of your colleagues. I will be visiting your company next week and would like to meet with you for about fifteen minutes so you can see the total scope of the work that I do."**

> **"Hi, this is ________________, and my name might be familiar to you because I've been working with some of your colleagues at (company) and speaking to them about the generous benefit package you receive. I'm a financial professional with (company), and my work focuses on helping people to understand their benefits and, more importantly, to see how they fit in with their family's needs. I'd like to find a time when we can meet for about fifteen minutes, and I can show you the total scope of the work I do and be an additional financial resource to you. What is generally the less hectic time in your work day—before or after lunch?"**

(Group) No-Cost Payroll-Deduction Plan

There are lots of companies that don't know about the virtues of group benefit plans. As I've said several times so far, the best route to the corporate decision makers is through the people who already know you (your clients or personal friends), and they will introduce you to them. In each of these scripts, you have to get to the right party so you can share that there really is a "virtually no cost benefit" they can offer their employees. Following are some scripts you can use:

> **"I specialize in helping small businesses reduce the cost of employee benefits. I have a program that will offer your employees a benefit at virtually no cost to you. It is very popular with the employees, and for a change, you become the hero."**

> **"I share information with businesses like yours about employee benefits, which can be provided at virtually no cost to you but is very popular with the employees. This idea has created a true win-win situation for many employers who are looking to reward their employees but always keep an eye on the bottom line."**

> **"I'm calling about some of the work we've done for companies like yours in the area of voluntary payroll-deduction programs. Perhaps you are aware of this trend. The attraction of this concept is that they are voluntary and the employees individually choose to participate and pay 100 percent of the premiums. They have simple administration and—most important—it's an opportunity to expand the current benefits program you currently offer with virtually no cost to you."**

RECRUITING

THE RECRUITING PHONE CALL MIRRORS THE ADVISOR CALL IN THAT YOUR GOAL is a face-to-face appointment. The primary flaw I hear when observing recruiting calls is that the recruiter starts to sell the job. The goal is to talk about the job in person, not on the phone. Therefore, these scripts present **the interview** as the opportunity—not the career.

Similar to advisors, recruiters are finding it harder to get candidates on the phone. I would recommend employing the same system of asking for the **Phone Date** rather than randomly dialing people who don't know you. If using resumé internet services, upon seeing a viable resumé, you should text a request for a **Phone Date** immediately. If you get referred to a candidate, do the same thing. Here is the text:

> **"I know that John Smith has told you a little bit about me and our career opportunity. I'd like to speak to you by phone, so send me some times you are available in the next two weeks for a brief call."**

Like advisors, recruiters should consider more face-to-face marketing. If you have stopped going to job fairs, you might want to rethink that decision. When meeting someone at a job fair, you want to share your digital business card and become a contact. Future communications are more likely to be picked up. With millennials, this is more important than ever.

Trying to schedule an interview right at the job fair would be a priority. If you don't have time or the ability to do so, exchange contact information followed by a text request for a **Phone Date.** The scripts below assume the **Phone Date** was scheduled and you've shared your digital business card.

Job Fair

> **"Hi, I'm glad we have a chance to talk again since we didn't get enough time to do that at the Job Fair at the Staples Center. You briefly told me that you were looking to find an entrepreneurial opportunity, and you probably remember that I'm with (company). I'd like to schedule an appointment so we can continue the conversation we started at the Job Fair. What is easier for you—earlier or later in the day?"**

> **"Hi, I'm glad we're having a second conversation because when we talked at the Job Fair, some things you said prompted me to reach out to you again. I understand that your career is in transition, and as the Sales Manager for (your company) here in (town) I'm always looking for exceptional people to expand our organization. I was thinking that we should meet to explore the career opportunity I have for either yourself or someone that you know. What is the better time for you during the day—the**

morning or afternoon?"

If you see a candidate with a resumé online, the following is a great script:

> **"Hi, this is ______________, and I look at resumés on line every day, but when I saw yours, I stopped. Your experience is similar to people who traditionally do very well in our business, but they are also people who often feel underpaid, underappreciated, or underutilized in their current career. I'd be interested in scheduling an initial appointment where you can find out more about the opportunity I have at my company and see if we might be able to fit whatever goal prompted you to put your resumeéon the internet. In general, would earlier or later in the day be better for you?"**

The best candidate is, of course, a referral. Get introduced by the nominator, which allows you to get into the candidate's phone and ask for a **Phone Date.** Then use this verbiage:

> **"Hi, it's nice to 'meet you' on the phone. When I got your name from (referring person), he/she told me that you were an intelligent and high-energy person and someone I might want to talk to. They also told me that you were open-minded and a curious person. Did they get that right? I told him/her that we're looking for people who might want to hear about other careers for a number of reasons; some of which are that they feel underpaid, or underappreciated, or want to be in their own business but don't want to "go-it-alone." If that sounds like you, we**

should schedule a meeting. What is the easiest time for you—earlier or later in the week?"

"Hi, it's nice to 'meet you' on the phone. When I was with (referring person) recently, he/she told me that you were an intelligent and high-energy person and someone I might want to talk to. Our company is looking for special individuals to expand our team, and when I profiled the ideal person, (referring person) immediately thought of you. I'd be interested in scheduling an initial appointment where you can find out more about the opportunity I have at my company. In general, would earlier or later in the day be better for you?"

"Hi, I'm glad we found a time to talk. When I was with (referring person) and told him/her about our opportunity, he/she mentioned you. Sometimes we get referred to people who suspect they will be downsized or moved out of their current position, and these people are at the point where they want to take control of their careers in a different way. At (referring person's) suggestion, I thought we should talk and see if we can set a time where I can learn more about your situation and tell you more about our company and see if there is any reason to take it further."

"I am calling you at the suggestion of (referring person). Recently, he/she told me that you might be interested in hearing about other career opportunities since your current situation might not be bringing you the kind of freedom and compensation you are looking for. (Referring

person) told me that you were an open-minded person and would at least want to know what our company offers. We are looking for a certain type of individual, and (referring person's) description of you and your successes makes me think that a brief meeting, at least, would be worthwhile for both of us."

There are occasions where you might meet an experienced advisor who is not as happy at his/her agency as they had hoped. Or you meet independent advisors who are now interested in more support and camaraderie. Here is a script for that scenario:

"Hi, this is ______, and I'm a sales director with (company) here in ______. The reason for my call is that I am looking for talented people who might be unsatisfied with their current company —or seeking a better support system. Typically, a good fit is someone who is goal-oriented, a team player, and a strong force in the financial industry looking for a place to rise to the top. Does that sound like you? I'm sure you are busy, but I'd like to sit down with you away from your office. In general, what would be a less-hectic time in your week—mornings or afternoons?"

Some agencies are focusing their recruiting efforts on women. Here's a script for that circumstance:

"The reason for my call is simple. I am building a powerhouse unit of women in the financial industry. I've done an incredible job creating a team of professional women in our organization, but I am looking for someone who's been in the financial industry and can help guide the path

of this team. I am looking for partnerships from women who have proven themselves or are looking for a chance to prove their abilities. Our office focuses on women and that means great resources are available for those who join us. I am sure you have a hectic week, so what would be best for you—a morning coffee or an afternoon discussion?"

If you've reached out to someone on **LinkedIn** and received a positive response from In Message to talk on the phone, here is some verbiage to consider:

"Hi, this is __________, and I am a recruiter for a large, well-known financial company here in __________. I look at bios on LinkedIn every day, and when I saw yours I immediately stopped. Your experience is similar to people who traditionally do very well in our business but they are also people who often feel underpaid, underappreciated, or underutilized in their current career. If this sounds like you, then I'm sure you'd be interested in scheduling an initial appointment where we can find out more about the opportunity I have at my company and see if we might be able to fit whatever career idea prompted you to put your resume on the internet."

RESPONSE HANDLING

In light of our current climate of smartphones, this book has discussed the challenges of reaching people and speaking to them in "real time." The marketing suggestions, plus the ideas of Becoming a Contact and setting **Phone Dates**, will help you to survive our no pick-up culture. However, the good news is that once you've attained a **Phone Date** and someone *does* pick up, your chances of getting an appointment are much, much higher than they used to be. Some of my groups report appointment-setting rates of 80 percent and better. Remember, once you're granted a **Phone Date**, the prospect or referral already knows who you are and what you do. So they're more likely to want the appointment. *Most refusals happen before you make the call.* Here is what now happens: someone doesn't respond to your request for a **Phone Date**—that's today's version of "I've got an advisor." Or, you start to communicate digitally and at some point, the other person disappears. That's today's version of "I'm not interested," commonly referred to as "ghosting."

Having said all this, my book would be incomplete if I didn't teach you how to handle a response that isn't a direct "yes."

The most common concern of financial professionals making calls is how they will respond to "an objection." Mentally changing the word "objection" to the word "problem" will prevent you from perceiving this as a battle. The prospect isn't *objecting* to getting together with you. They are sharing a reality in their lives that prevents them from seeing the value of the appointment. If your script is missing a benefit (the F statement), problems will arise more often.

The best way to handle a problem is to be prepared. You need a structured way of handling all of them. Ad-libbing every answer, and talking too much, will not work.

A well-known technique for handling problems is what's known as "Feel-Felt-Found," which provides a consistent, easy-to-remember verbal structure. Most strategies for phoning require updating, and "Feel-Felt-Found" does, too.

The *structure* of the technique works because essentially you are doing the following:

- **Acknowledging** what the client said and expressing your respect for it.
- **Grouping them** with other people who have had the same concern.
- **Sharing with them** how those people **still met with you** and found the appointment to be **beneficial**.

It's the third statement that requires you to insert a benefit that must be specific to the problem. (e.g. if a person says, "I already have an advisor," your benefit needs to relate to that). Instead of sticking to the exact wording of the traditional feel-felt-found, here on the facing page is a more modern option:

1. *I can appreciate your telling me that.*

   Alternates: *I hear what you're saying* **OR** *I understand.*

2. *Other people initially said that to me, too .*

   Change to: *I hear that a lot.*

3. *But they found after meeting with me that . . .*

It is important to keep sentence #3 the same, and then insert the related benefits suggested. Again, if you don't practice, you will sound awkward. You want to practice this language so you sound natural when speaking with a prospect. Remember: This isn't a battle between you and the prospect.

Here is one completed response handler:

"I don't have enough money to meet with an advisor."

"I hear what you're saying, and many people are struggling with their finances at this time. But they found, after meeting with me, that the work that I do is about organizing your money, not necessarily spending more. I'd like to see if I can do that for you. With that in mind, what is less hectic for you—this week or next?"

This problem is one of the most common statements you'll hear when you offer an appointment. The ones for which I've chosen to show examples are the most frequent. If you hear something that sounds odd, it usually is. Make enough calls in your career and if something sounds weird, it *is weird*! (If it waddles like a duck, quacks like a duck . . . it's a duck!)

The *most* common response the advisors report to me is:

"I've already got an advisor."

or:

"I have been working with someone for a long time."

There are two really good answers to this:

"I hear what you're saying, and I'd be shocked if someone in your position had never worked with a financial professional. However, most of my clients found, after they met me, that since no one person has the cornerstone on all the good ideas, I might offer you something that complements your existing portfolio. I think it's worth seeing if I can do that for you. Sound fair enough? With that in mind, what is easier for you, earlier or later in the day?"

My **favorite answer** to "I've got a financial person already" is the following one. You need to memorize it and own it.

"I understand, and most of my clients had already worked with someone else when they met me. But I will make you two promises. One, I will never undo any good work another advisor has done for you; and two, I will only make suggestions that will enhance or complement your current portfolio. With this as the premise for a cup of coffee, what is less hectic for you—earlier or later in the week?"

If you find yourself mingling with busy business owners, you're going to find it hard to get appointments with them. There might be more rescheduling with CEO's, business owners, certain professionals, etc. Be patient. But also use this answer to let them know most of your clients are busy people.

Suppose on the phone the client says, "I'm really busy now."

"I hear you and most of my clients are super-busy people. They also found, after meeting with me, that the role I take

in my client's lives involves freeing up time for them by putting their concerns about their money on my shoulders. I'd like to show you how I work. What is less hectic for you—earlier or later in the day?"

Alternative:

"They found after meeting with me that the information I share with them could actually free up time they previously spent thinking or worrying about their money."

A difficult time of year for all professionals is the holiday season. You might find it harder to get your clients to meet with you, even when it's important to make certain decisions before the end of the calendar year. Three suggested responses follow. Depending on your client's major reason for putting off the meeting, choose the one that you believe will work best.

Too stressed out by the holidays to find time for an appointment:

"I hear you, and most of my clients are pretty stressed out at this time of year, but they found after meeting with me that a coffee appointment (or lunch) with me was the one break they could look forward to in the middle of the chaos. I'd like to do that for you. Where should we meet—at Starbucks or Dunkin' Donuts?" (or a choice of two restaurants)

Too much going on with their family (e.g., out-of-towners coming, getting their house ready):

"I understand, and many of my clients are in that exact situation. But they found after meeting with me that they were glad that they did since this is a time to be thinking about family. Our conversation was, in fact, about providing for your family. I think you'll find that having our appointment now makes a lot of sense. When should we get together—earlier or later this week?"

If a business person is putting you off:

"I hear you, and most of my business clients are finding this time of year very stressful and busy. But they found after meeting with me that some of the ideas that we might explore could be calendar sensitive, and to discuss them now would be timely. I think it's important enough to schedule before the end of the year. What's easier for you—this week or next?"

Here are a few more standard responses you might encounter:

"Email me something."

"I hear you and some of my clients initially think that an email will be sufficient. But they found after meeting with me that because information is usually so generic, but their financial lives are so specific, a face-to-face meeting is far more beneficial." (Close)

"The market is too volatile."

"I understand what you're saying and other clients thought that now was not a good time to meet due to the market fluctuations, but they found after talking with me that it was comforting to speak to a financial professional to make sure they're doing all they can in this market." (Close)

"I have a family member who takes care of this."

"I hear you and have met other people who initially worked with people in their family. But they found, after a visit with me, that—in fact—they were more comfortable speaking about their finances with me because I *wasn't* a family member. You may find that to be true as well." (close)

APPENDIX: ALL SCRIPTS

Social Event Follow-up

Emailed/Texted for a Phone Date:

"Hi, John, (small talk about event at Sam and Ellen's). I noticed that when we were talking, you had said you were concerned about keeping your most valuable executives at your company without literally tying them to their chairs. I had mentioned that I've worked with other CEO's in the same situation and wanted to find a time to go for either coffee or lunch so I can expand on that with you. What's generally easier for you, earlier or later in the week?"

"Hi, John, it's Gail. (small talk about the event where you met—keep under two minutes). I'm looking at my calendar for next week. What's a good day for us to meet for coffee—or lunch, if you prefer?"

Natural Market

Group #1: For New Advisors:

"Hi, this is _______ , and I'm sure that you've heard about my new career with (name of your company). I'm really excited about it and the reason I've called is that I would like to position myself—and my team*—as an additional financial resource to you. I'd like to set a time when we can get together so that I can share with you the total scope of the work that we do. That way, you can use my team, our expertise, and the resources of our company any way that makes you feel the most comfortable. With that in mind, what is less hectic—days or evenings?"

*(If you bring your manager with you on your appointments, using "my team" and the pronoun "we" is important.)

"I wanted to let you know that I started a career as (an agent, financial advisor) at (company), and I decided I am going to build my practice around the people I care about the most. In fact, they asked us to list those people and, of course, you were on the top of my list. I'd like to position myself as a financial resource to you and find a time when I can show you the new scope of the work that I do, and then you can use me and all the resources at my disposal, in any way that makes you feel the most comfortable."

"I don't know if you've heard, but I've become involved in a new career that I'm really excited about, and I wanted to call you to share my news. I've joined (company) and I'm focusing my work on helping the people I know best to address their financial goals. At this juncture, I simply would like to position myself and my team as an additional financial resource to you and spend some time together to show you the total scope of the work that we do. That way, you can use me and all the resources we have in any way that makes the most sense to you."

Group #1: For Experienced Advisors:
Apology Script:
"John, I'm so glad I bumped in to you because I need to tell you that I owe you an apology. (Pause and let them hear what you just said.) You know that I have been in financial services for more than ________ years, and in all that time, I've never reached out to you on a professional basis, and I need to rectify that. I would like to be an additional financial resource to you, and I want us to get together so that I can share with you the total scope of the work that I do. That way, you will be better able to use my expertise any way that makes you feel the most comfortable. I know you're usually very busy; when can we go for coffee or lunch?"

"Hello, this is ______________. As you know, I have been in financial services for more than ________ years, and in all that time, I've never called you on a professional basis, and I am rectifying that with this phone call. I would like to position myself as an additional financial resource to you, and I'm calling to set a time for us to get together so that I can share with you the total scope of the work that I do. That way, you will be better able to use my expertise any way that makes you feel the most comfortable. With that in mind, when would you like to meet—this week or next?"

"Hi, it's (your name). I'm calling you because I feel that I have been professionally irresponsible in that I have never called you and offered you my assistance in my professional capacity. I would like to position myself as an additional financial resource to you. In order for you to best figure out how to do that, I'd like to get together and share with you the total scope of the work that I do. That way, you'll be able to use my experience and knowledge any way you see fit. When can I take you out for a cup of coffee—this week or next?"

Group #2: Acquaintances, Friends, Vendors:
"Hi, this is _______, and I'm sure that you've heard about my new career with (company). I'm really excited about it, and the reason I've called is that I would like to position myself—and my team—as an additional financial resource to you. I'd like to set a time when we could get together so that we* can share with you the total scope of the work that we do. That way, you can use me, my team, and the resources of our company in any way that makes you feel the most comfortable. With that in mind, what is less hectic—days or evenings?"
(Change the pronouns back to "me' or "my' if you are experienced and don't work on a team.)

Business Owners You Know:
"The reason I'm calling is that I've made a career switch to (company), and I was in a business concepts class the other day and thought of you. They were discussing ideas that can save a small business owner like you important money, enough that it would affect your bottom line. I would like to schedule an appointment to talk to you briefly about these ideas because if I were able to show you how to save money in your business, I'd certainly like to do that."

"Last week I was sitting with a client with a business just like yours, and I thought of you. I wanted to give you a call because, in my financial practice, my primary focus has been on assisting (professionals and/or) business owners in enhancing their personal (and business) financial position. I'd like to get together and show you some of the ideas I shared with my other business client."

Recalling Your Natural Market:
"I was sitting in a class that was primarily about (small businesses, young families saving for college, a subject of interest to them), and I kept thinking of you. I wanted to call and invite you to join me for a cup of coffee so that I can give you some of these really terrific ideas that I have learned. I felt that would be neglecting you if I didn't share them."

Overhearing Financial Concerns:
"Hi, this is__________. We recently were at (event), and I overheard you mentioning a concern about (example: paying for college, paying for benefits, the current economy). Because I am a financial professional, I hear those kinds of comments with a different ear, and so the reason for my call today is to position myself as an additional financial resource. I'd like to schedule a time when we can sit down, and I can show you the total scope of the work that I do, and you can then decide how you might like to use me and all my resources."

"Hi, this is _____, and we were at (event), and during a discussion you said that you were concerned about ________. As a financial professional, I hear those kinds of comments differently, so it motivated me to call you. I'd like to offer to position myself as an additional resource to you and your family/business and get together so I can show you the total scope of the work that I do. Then you can use me and all my resources in any way that feels most comfortable to you."

Transitioning Experienced Advisors:
"Hi, this is __________________ (from old company if appropriate). I don't know if you've heard, but I have made a lateral move in my career, and I have partnered with a terrific organization, ________. I did this because I thought it would be good for me and good for you. I would like to get together with you to show you the new scope of the work that I now do, and I am sure that I will be a more effective financial resource to you in my new capacity."

Group #3:
"Hi, it's ____________, and it's been a while! I'm calling to find a time to get together for lunch or coffee so we can catch up. I'd like to know what you've been doing (how your family is, etc.) and let you know what's been going on with me as well. What's easier for you—this week or next?"

Group #4 and Group #5:
"Hi, this is _____, and I'm calling you for help with my business. I don't know if you heard that I have joined (company), and I'm pretty excited about it. I know that you are very successful, and I wanted to set a time when I can visit with you and show you our process to get your opinion on it. For the privilege of picking your brain, I'd like to buy you breakfast/lunch. And I know you're busy, so what is the least hectic day for you—earlier or later in the week?"

Agency-Sponsored Seminar:

"Hi, Aunt Betty. I'm calling for two reasons. First (ask a personal question that is specific to her life, not a general "How are you?", which can lead to a tangent). The other reason for my call is that my firm is sponsoring a really interesting workshop, and when I heard about it, I immediately thought of you. It's about (brief description), and I thought you and Uncle John would really want to hear this information. The event is on (day, time, date), and since we are serving a meal, they've asked us to get an accurate head count. I'd like to save two seats for you."

Advisor Seminars

Invite Call:

"Hello, this is _______ with _________. I'm calling to follow up on an invitation I recently sent you. It was about our upcoming workshop on _________. Many of my clients have expressed a concern and interest in this topic, so I've decided to offer more information in a public arena. I think this topic is one that relates to *our* conversations. I'm keeping the seating limited so that we can allow for questions. How many seats would you like us to save for you?"

Invitation Follow-up for Client Invitation:

"Hello, this is _______ with _________. I'm calling to follow up on an invitation we sent you to our upcoming workshop on ________. Many of my clients have expressed a concern and interest in this topic, so I've decided to offer more information in a public arena. I think this topic is one that relates to *our* conversations. I'm keeping the seating limited so that we can keep the group small enough for questions. How many seats would you like us to save for you?"

After Seminar—Expressed Interest in an Appointment:
"Hello, this is ________. At our Workshop on ________, you indicated that you were interested in a private consultation/appointment so we can personalize the information for you. I'd be happy to visit with you to do that. Where is the best place for us to meet—your home or my office?"

Invited to Seminar—Didn't/Couldn't Attend:
"I am following up with those who were unable to attend our (title) workshop and offering to get together with you to discuss some of the highlights of the program. If we can schedule a time—either at your home or my office—I can give you an abbreviated version of the program, and personalize it to your situation."

Trade Show Follow-up:
"Hi, John, it's Gail Goodman. We met briefly at the (trade show) but didn't have enough time to really find out more about each other's business. I'd like to continue our conversation and wanted to find out what would be the best time for coffee. I'd be happy to meet you at the closest Starbucks, or, if your week is hectic, I can bring you some caffeine when you need it. Which one sounds better?"

Referrals

Introduced by a Referrer:
"Hi, this is ______________. Good to meet you on the phone, and John speaks very highly of you. I'd like to schedule a time to share with you the total scope of the financial work that I do, and then you can see why (John) suggested that we meet. Generally, what's easier for you—earlier or later in the day?"

Not Introduced by a Referrer:

"Hi, this is _______________, and a friend/colleague of yours (referring person), suggested that I give you a call. (Referring person) is not only a friend of mine, but she is also my client. I'm with (company), and we recently met, and I did some very good financial work with (referring person), and she wanted me to call you. All I would like to do at this point is position myself as an additional financial resource to you and schedule a time when I can share with you the total scope of the work that I do. That way, you can use me in any way that makes you feel comfortable."

"Hi, this is _______, and a mutual friend suggested I give you a call. Harry Smith is both my friend and client, and I am his financial advisor—and he speaks very highly of you. I am with (company) and recently, we met to discuss some ideas for (himself, his employees, whatever works here), and he thought that some of the concepts I shared with him might interest you. What I'd like to do is get together, show you the total scope of the work I do, and then you can use me in any way that makes you most comfortable."

If a Center of Influence Has Introduced You:

"Hi, this is___________, and recently, I was with (COI), and he suggested I give you a call. (COI) and I are friends and we were talking about our businesses, and as a financial professional with (company) he thought I could position myself as an additional financial resource to you/your business. I'd like to find a time when we can meet for a cup of coffee, and I can share with you the scope of the work that I do, which will allow you to figure out the best way to use both myself and all the resources of my company."

If You Have Been Referred to a Possible Center of Influence:
"Hello, this is ___________, and I was referred to you by (referring person), and the reason I was calling is that I am looking for other professionals who can provide complementary services to my clients. I only give my clients Cadillac service, and I am looking for other professionals who pride themselves on doing the same thing. (Referrer) thought you were that type of person and told me to call you. So I'd like to set up a time for us to get together and discuss the possibility of pooling our resources for the benefit of our potential mutual clients."

Calling a Potential Center of Influence You Know:
"Hi, this is ___________, and I'm calling because in my financial practice I am often in a position to need the services of an attorney/accountant, and I immediately thought of you. What I'd like to do is find a time when we can sit and talk in more detail about our respective practices and see if there is a basis for us to consider doing some referring to the other's clients."

Calling the Referral from a Center of Influence:
(Try to get your contact information sent in advance.)
"Hi, this is ___________, and I was recently with (COI), and he/she suggested that I give you a call. (COI) and I are colleagues and frequently will find that our clients need the services of the other. That is the reason for my call. I am a financial advisor with (company), and I work with people on (financial issue that is appropriate for this client.) (COI) suggested that we schedule a time to sit down, and I can share with you the scope of the work that I do and see how, along with (COI), I can be part of your professional team."

Association Member:
"Hello, Mr./Ms. Business, this is (name) calling from (company). Our name is probably familiar to you because we have an alliance with (association) and are the approved provider for different benefits for the members. You have probably seen the letter from (association) announcing this relationship. I'd like to find a time when the two of us can sit down, and I will show you the scope of the work that we do for (association)'s business owners, and you can see how we're sharing creative ideas for their benefits program. What is the easiest time for us to spend (XX) minutes—earlier or later in the day?"

Orphan Calls:
"Hi, this is _______ calling from the local office of (your company), and I'm calling with good news! (*Pause*) I'm pleased to tell you that we have inherited each other. * The company has asked me to be your servicing agent, but right now you and I have a problem. You are a name on a manila folder (or computer screen), and I am a strange voice over the phone. I can't do business this way, so I'd like to buy you a cup of coffee so that we can both put a face to the name. What would be easier for you—meeting at a Starbucks, your home or my office?"
*Here is where you laugh.

"I'm calling with great news! *(Pause)* We have inherited each other.* However, you and I have a problem. Right now, you are a name on a manila folder, and I am a strange voice over the phone. Since it makes me uncomfortable to service your account when I wouldn't even recognize you if we were to bump into each other at the grocery store, I'd like to schedule a time when we can get together—maybe for a cup of coffee—so we can both put a face to the name and be more comfortable with each other." (close)
*Here is where you laugh.

Staff Person:
"Hi, (client), this is ________, and I work with (agent) at (company) in (town).
"I have good news! We have inherited each other.* (*Pause*) The company has asked (agent) to be your servicing agent. We would like to give you the best service possible, but right now we can't do that when you are just a name on a manila folder to us, and we are a strange voice over the phone to you. ____________ would like to schedule a time when you can meet—maybe for a cup of coffee, so that you can both put a face to the name."

Calling Your Mentor's C+D Clients:
"Hello, this is (name), and I am (older agent's name)'s associate. You probably are aware that (older agent) isn't someone who makes unnecessary calls, but at this juncture, he's/she's asked me to call you. From time to time it makes sense to sit down with one of us and reassess some of the financial decisions you've made. One thing we know for certain is that things change—either your family situation or the market. I'd like to make sure that the programs you have in place are still working in line with your financial goals. I'm happy to drive to your house, or you are always invited to visit our offices. Which is better for you?"

Financial-Literacy Programs

Outreach Community Group Reach:
"Hi, ______________, I've been reaching out to other (insert type of organizations) in (town) to offer a financial wellness program as a service to the community. It is an educational experience, with the goal of helping participants to have better control over their financial life. I'd like to find a time where you have 20 to 30 minutes so I can show you

the curriculum that we've developed. Our research has found that financially educated people are happier and more productive, which is better for the overall community. What is less hectic for you—mornings or afternoons?"

Referral:

"Hello ______, this is ________ with (company) here in (town). I was referred to you by __________. He/She thinks very highly of you and your organization and recommended I reach out to you. Our firm conducted a financial literacy program for (referring person) and he/she thought we should share it with you as well. I'd like to find a time to sit down and share the details of the curriculum, which focuses on both individuals and families. In our research, we have found that the lack of financial literacy is wreaking havoc in America today. (Referrer) suggested we get together to see how it fits into your organization. I know you're very busy, but what is less hectic for you, mornings or afternoons?"

Business:

"Hi, this is _________, and I am with (company), and I am calling because our company is providing a free financial-literacy program to local businesses. The seminar is designed for large (or small, whichever you're calling) companies that want to provide an educational benefit to their employees, and it's no cost to you. I would like to schedule a brief meeting to further show you the details of the program. Most employers would agree that financially educated and prepared employees means a happier, more productive workforce. In general, what is the less hectic time for you—before or after lunch?"

"I'm following up on an email I recently sent you regarding our corporate financial-planning programs. I work with many benefits coordinators in providing a value-added service to your company, at no charge to you and with little work on your part. I'd like to set up a mutually convenient time when I can show you the benefits of having corporate-sponsored, financial-planning seminars for your employees. The win-win arrangement is that we do all the work and you get all the credit."

Congregation Leader:
"I wanted to speak to you about setting up a time when we can discuss my helping our church/temple with an improved charitable giving program. There are several ways we can set it up so that the outcome is a clear win-win situation—there is more money for our congregation, but in addition there are tax benefits for the giver. These programs have been very successful in other churches/temples, and I'd like to see ours get the same increase in generous donations."

Target Markets:
"I specialize in working with florists since my family has been in the floral business for forty years, and I am familiar with the cyclical nature of the business. I have been able to sit down with other florists and assist in identifying appropriate concepts and ideas to meet their current or future goals."

"As a former restaurant manager, I have focused my current work in the financial-services industry on helping my colleagues in the food business to be able to meet their financial goals. What I would like to do is visit with you and briefly discuss some of the financial programs that I believe meet the unique needs of restaurant owners. In this short visit, we can get to know each other, and then if you think my ideas are helpful, we can take it from there."

"Being a former manufacturer, I have focused my current work in the insurance and investment industry on providing ideas to executives in the garment center. These concepts are designed to help them handle their unique problems associated with cash flow, retirement, and other serious financial challenges. I would like to share some ideas that I think you will find helpful to achieve the financial success you deserve."

"The last time we spoke, as you might recall, I was helping military families build a successful financial future. I am now working with (company) because it gives me the ability to be a financial resource to my friends who are in the service. I would love to sit down with you and (spouse) to show you the total scope of the work I'm doing, and then you can decide how to best use all of our resources."

Retirement-Planning Specialist:

Clients:

"Hi, ____________________, it's me. I'm calling for two reasons. (Ask a personal question about their life, and let this part of the conversation continue for a couple of minutes.) The other reason for my call is that I haven't spoken to you on a professional basis about the work my firm does for companies with retirement plans. I know you provide such a plan to your employees, and I'd be remiss if I didn't share with you some of the services and ideas that I've been sharing with people who are not my (friends/relatives). The unique approach we have is that we work from a service-oriented model. First, we analyze a variety of fees that can easily get expensive for the company. In addition, our goal is to protect the person with the fiduciary responsibility for the plan, making sure they are audit-ready at all times. I'd like to have a face-to-face meeting with you and the other executives who are in charge of your plan. What is less hectic for you—generally—earlier or later in the week?"

"Hi, ________________, it's (name). I'm calling for two reasons. First, I wanted to briefly talk about (product, form, whatever reason you would call them—even a personal one). The other reason for my call is that I recently did some work with a client who has a retirement plan very similar to yours. I have been remiss in not telling you that I have access to a variety of resources to help you with your company plan as well. Without going into a lot of detail right now, I'd like to schedule a meeting in which I can describe the analysis we do on a variety of features of a retirement plan. I know your days are busy, so I'd be happy to schedule a time early in the morning before things get too hectic."

For Clients Who Can Refer You Within Their Company:
"Hi, ________________, it's (name). I'm calling for two reasons. First, I wanted to briefly talk about (product, form, whatever reason you would call them). The other reason for my call is that I know that at (their company) you are participating in the retirement plan. Our firm has an exclusive division that works with the people who are in charge of plans like yours. The way your retirement plan is managed can have an impact on your own portion of it. I would like to speak to the person in charge of your plan, but I would need you to introduce me to them."

Corporate Nesting:
"I do a lot of work with (their company) employees in helping them to assess their current benefits package, especially their retirement plan. Most plans only provide an 800 number for employees to get personalized information, and I would like to position myself as an additional financial resource to you as I've done with some of your colleagues. I will be visiting your company next week and would like to meet with you for about fifteen minutes so you can see the total scope of the work that I do."

"Hi, this is ______________, and my name might be familiar to you because I've been working with some of your colleagues at (company) and speaking to them about the generous benefit package you receive. I'm a financial professional with (company), and my work focuses on helping people to understand their benefits and, more importantly, to see how they fit in with their family's needs. I'd like to find a time when we can meet for about fifteen minutes, and I can show you the total scope of work I do and be an additional financial resource to you. What is generally the less hectic time in your work day—before or after lunch?"

No-Cost Payroll Deduction:
"I specialize in helping small businesses reduce the cost of employee benefits. I have a program that will offer your employees a benefit at virtually no cost to you. It is very popular with the employees, and for a change, you become the hero."

"I share information with businesses like yours about employee benefits, which can be provided at virtually no cost to you but is very popular with the employees. This idea has created a true win-win situation for many employers who are looking to reward their employees but always keeping an eye on costs."

"I'm calling about some of the work we've done for companies like yours in the area of voluntary payroll-deduction programs. Perhaps you are aware of this trend. The attraction of this concept is that they are voluntary, and the employees individually chose to participate and pay 100 percent of the premiums; they have simple administration and—most important—it's an opportunity to expand the benefits program you currently offer with virtually no cost to you."

RESOURCES

Michael Goldberg—Knockout Networking
Michael@KONetworking.com
knockoutnetworking.com

Andrea Nierenberg—Nierenberg Consulting Group, LLC
andrea@nierenberggroup.com
Nierenberggroup.com

ABOUT THE AUTHOR

If you hear the phrase "The PhoneTeacher," that's Gail Goodman. She's well known in financial services because she has trained more than 70,000 financial professionals. Gail's career has been devoted to helping salespeople schedule face-to-face appointments with new prospects.

For more than three decades, Gail has continually adapted her training and materials to reflect our ever-changing environment. Despite the rise of technology, the human voice cannot be replaced. Initially, phones were our primary appointment-setting tool, but today's paradigm is "The Digital-Vocal-Personal Mix." Salespeople and managers need to know how to synthesize technology, phone calling, and face-to-face opportunities into a more modern way of approaching prospects.

Gail's training combines on-site seminars, phone role-playing sessions, videos, webinars, audio programs, and one-on-one coaching to increase the salesperson's ability to sit down with a new potential client.

Gail lives on a horse farm outside of Nashville with her husband and too many animals.

Made in the USA
Monee, IL
18 November 2020